FAMILY AND CONSUMER SCIENCE LIFEPAC 4
THE CLOTHES YOU WEAR

CONTENTS

S0-AGI-300

Author: Marcia Parker, M.Ed.
Editor: Alan Christopherson, M.S.
Illustrations: Alpha Omega Graphics

Alpha Omega Publications®

804 N. 2nd Ave. E., Rock Rapids, IA 51246-1759
© MM by Alpha Omega Publications, Inc.   All rights reserved.
LIFEPAC is a registered trademark of Alpha Omega Publications, Inc.

THE CLOTHES YOU WEAR

What is the purpose of clothing? The first mention of clothes in the Bible is found in Genesis 3:7 when Adam and Eve, "...made themselves aprons" to cover and protect themselves. This LIFEPAC® will discuss the purposes for making specific choices of clothes.

It is important to have a basic understanding of fashion cycles, clothing construction, and clothing business terms in order to make informed choices when selecting your wardrobe. Understanding the elements and principles of design and garment styles will help you make wise selections that will compliment your body type.

Clothing is seasonal, cultural, and personal, but textiles and fabrics influence your choices accordingly. For example, you wouldn't wear wool in the summer—you would be extremely warm if you did. Knowing whether a garment is made from a natural or man-made fabric is important in its care. It is also important to select the proper fabric when making a garment.

The last section will address the topic of caring for clothing. You will be able to demonstrate techniques in mending and laundering your clothes. Clothes will last a long time if they are properly cared for. Mending clothing as soon as problems are discovered keeps them from becoming worse. Properly laundering clothes not only insures a longer-lasting garment but enhances its appearance as well.

OBJECTIVES

Read these objectives. The objectives tell you what you will be able to do when you have successively completed this LIFEPAC.

When you have finished this LIFEPAC, you should be able to:

1. Identify the purposes for making specific choices in clothes.

2. Gain a basic understanding of fashion cycles.

3. Define fashion terms, clothing construction terms, and clothing business terms that affect your wardrobe selections.

4. Analyze your present wardrobe and design a plan to gradually improve it.

5. Gain an understanding of the elements and principles of design.

6. Identify different garment styles.

7. Identify your body type for making proper clothing choices.

8. Identify various types of both natural and man-made fabrics.

9. Demonstrate various mending techniques.

10. Demonstrate the ability to launder clothing.

I. FASHION

The clothing worn by the ancient Hebrews was significant. Clothing worn by the Hebrews served as the external symbol of the individual's innermost feelings and desires. Festive and joyful occasions called for bright colors, while the Jew in mourning put on sackcloth, the poorest kind of dress. One's status in society also determined the manner of dress. Clothes play an important role in our lives as well; wearing the appropriate **attire** for every occasion or activity is a testimony of character and an expression of individuality.

Avoid fads—you don't have to be "in style" to be stylish. Keep a sharp wardrobe, choosing classic styles in quality fabrics that flatter your body type. Knowing about fashion is important so that you can make proper choices in the selection of your wardrobe. An understanding of the elements and principles of design and garment styles will help you improve your present wardrobe and make those wise choices.

SECTION OBJECTIVES

Review these objectives. When you have completed this section, you should be able to:

1. Identify the purposes for making specific choices in clothes.

2. Gain a basic understanding of fashion cycles.

3. Define fashion terms, clothing construction terms, and clothing business terms that affect your wardrobe selections.

4. Analyze your present wardrobe and design a plan for gradually improving it.

THE PURPOSE OF CLOTHING

People wear clothing for protection. The Jewish *simlah* was an outer garment resembling a large sheet with a hood, used for additional warmth.[1] We too use clothing for protection from the **elements**: raincoats, sweaters, coats, hats, gloves, sunglasses, etc. Clothes also protect us from occupational hazards such as safety helmets for construction workers, fire-retardant suits for firefighters, lab coats for scientists, and latex gloves for doctors. On a more domestic level, the apron protects clothes while cooking. Clothes also serve to protect our bodies from harm such as helmets and bulletproof vests.

Another reason for wearing clothing is to cover parts of the body that society feels should be covered. Dress modestly. Most of today's fads do not promote modesty (low necklines, high hem lines, tight-fitting tops, tight-fitting jeans/pants or jeans/pants that hang way below the belt line), heavily **accentuating** the body rather than the face. Be conscious to design your wardrobe to focus attention on your **countenance** rather than your body.

Clothes also express status or one's position or rank in comparison to others. Status is reflected when one's clothes give a person a higher social rank, acceptance and peer approval by identifying him according to wealth, employment, and social level. Thus, a person is often labeled according to how she dresses: a banker, a lawyer, a doctor, a nurse, a soldier, a construction worker, a farmer, an inmate, a

---

1. Packer, J.I., Tenney Merrill C. and White, William, Jr., *The Bible Almanac*, Thomas Nelson Publishers, 1980. p475

rock musician, a gang member, or an athlete. All of these people walk different paths in life, yet all wear a **uniform**, service stripes, badge, or clothes that clearly identify his/her status or role to others. The Hebrews did the same. The *kethon* was the costume of the common people, the *beged* was a badge of dignity to the wearer (worn by distinguished members of great families), and the *addereth* was worn to indicate that the wearer was a person of importance.[2]

Clothes are also used to symbolize feelings. Again, the Hebrews utilized certain kinds of cloth with astonishingly vivid colors of white, purple, scarlet, blue, yellow, and black to represent the state of their minds and emotions. When joyful and ready to enter into festive occasions, they donned their clothing of brightest array. When they mourned or humbled themselves, they put on sackcloth (literally, cloth from which sacks were made), which was considered the very poorest kind of dress, indicative of their lowly feelings. The Hebrews wore different types of clothing for special occasions: robes of honor, wedding garments, mourning garments, winter clothing.[3] Many of the Hebrew traditions have been carried on to us today. We wear black or at least subdued colors to funerals, and have special wedding garments as well. We have bright and elaborate clothes for festive occasions. Of course, we have special clothes for work and play. When planning a wardrobe, it is crucial to find proper clothes for all occasions.

We also wear clothes for adornment. It is a decoration through which we use color, line, shape, and texture to enhance our natural **beauty** and charm. Clothing items for body adornment also show how different cultures view beauty. For example, in Greece and Scotland men have traditionally worn short skirts. However, men in the United States would frequently be ridiculed for such attire.

Regardless of culture, two principles must be kept in mind:

1. *Individuality* — We are made in God's image, yet each is unique and different.
2. *Character* — We should do all things to the best of our abilities to honor God.

The clothing you select is a reflection of your character and individuality. Therefore, dress modestly. A girl should dress so that her entire countenance is feminine, a "softening" in line. She should shun harshness, sloppiness, or manliness. On the other hand, a boy should dress so as to enhance his masculinity, avoiding anything that makes him appear feminine.

Individuality is self-expression which distinguishes one person from another. Clothes which look good on one person may be a disaster on another. Although a person may have to **conform** to certain **dress codes** for church, work, or school, there are still ways to express individuality. You can select your own colors, lines, textures, and shapes and still remain within the boundaries set forth. **Accessories** are important to any wardrobe. If used correctly, you can even express your individuality even while wearing a uniform.

2.   *ibid.*, p. 475
3.   *ibid.*, p. 475-486

Personality is the sum total of characteristics that distinguish an individual, especially his or her behavioral or emotional tendencies. Your **attitudes** and **values** stem from your personality and are expressed through your dress. Values are the ideas, beliefs, or things that are important to someone. Different people have different values, such as believing that comfort, economy, easy care, prestige or the latest fashion look is specifically important. Attitudes are a person's feelings about or reactions to people, things, or ideas as formed from the person's values. We base our "**first impressions**" of people on our own values and attitudes. Sometimes these are correct, but often they are uninformed and unfair. However, it is wise to make a good first impression on someone else. What one wears to a job interview could very well be one deciding factor in whether or not that individual gets the position. The values and attitudes influencing a person's clothing choices change as he/she goes through life.

Not only does your personality determine what you choose to wear, but what you wear can also influence your personality. Wearing business attire often influences people to act more formally. On the other hand, casual attire produces a casual attitude and behavior.

Consider your lifestyle when selecting your wardrobe. What section of the country do you live in? Do you live in the city or the country? Does your life center on school, home, or work? Are you a busy socialite or a homebody?

The better you look, the better you feel about yourself and others. The better you look, the better others think about you, too. It is more difficult to respond well to someone who looks sloppy rather than one who looks and smells nice.

Fill in the blanks.

1.1 Give two examples of clothing that protects us from the climate. a. _____ b. _____

1.2 An asbestos suit for a fire fighter would be a good example of protective clothing that protects him/her from _____ .

1.3 It is important to be considerate of the feelings of others in society so dress _____ .

1.4 One's wardrobe should be designed to focus attention on the _____ rather than the body.

1.5 Define status. _____

1.6 Status is gained when clothing is able to give a person a _____ .

1.7 Define *identification*. _____

1.8 Give an example of how a person can be identified through his dress. _____

_____

1.9 In Hebrew culture, the _____ was the costume of the common people and the _____ was worn to indicate the importance of a person.

1.10 If the Hebrews were feeling lowly or in mourning, they wore _____ .

1.11 If the Hebrews were feeling festive they wore garments of what colors? _____

_____

1.12 Clothing worn as an adornment shows how different _____ view beauty.

1.13 The clothing you select is a reflection of your _____ and _____ .

4

1.14 Define *dress code*. _____

1.15 Define *personality*. _____

FASHION KNOWLEDGE

Fashion is "whatever is favored at a given time by those who are regarded as up-to-date" (Compton). Most often associated with clothes, it is also is used in reference to interior decoration, furniture, architecture, entertainment, etc.

Fashion changes from season to season and from year to year. It may even return to a style that was popular years before. The following are the stages of a typical fashion cycle.

1. New fashions are introduced and worn by fashion leaders.
2. Adaptations are worn by different people (styles are created in materials that everyone can afford).
3. Well-established style leads to mass acceptance.
4. Social saturation—everyone has it.
5. Overused, becomes dull and boring.
6. Declines in popularity.
7. Eventually becomes obsolete—no one will wear it.
8. In about 20 years, the fashion will be revived. Examples: flare legs on jeans (bell bottoms), boots, platform shoes.
9. Some changes from before, but the style is there and the fashion leaders wear them. (Thus the cycle begins again.)

The extent and duration of fashion cycles have been influenced by changes in technology. When clothing had to be handmade, fashions lasted for decades. Kings and especially queens greatly influenced the styles worn. However, the mass-production of a single design has greatly reduced the amount of time it takes for a style to reach large numbers of people. The mass media (books, plays, motion pictures, etc.) are now the dominant force in world-wide fashions. Thus, designs can go in and out of fashion much more quickly. The once popular book, *Little Lord Fauntleroy*, by Frances Hodgson Burnett introduced the velvet suit to young boys because the small hero in the story wore one! Important events changing the lifestyles of a society also influence the styles of the times. During World War II, women worked in factories and needed simple, easy-to-maintain dresses and even slacks, thus changing the fashions.[4]

The three **silhouettes** that were the basis for fashion cycles in the past were the bell, back fullness, and tubular silhouette. The bell silhouette has a fitted waist and full skirt. The back fullness silhouette has extra fullness that puffs out in the back only. The tubular silhouette is a slim and straight skirt all around with a high or low waistline.

back fullness

bell

tubular

4. *Compton's* Encyclopedia Online, "Clothing"; "Fashion"; "Dress Design"

5

Parisian designers have been the major influence on women's fashions while the Bond Street tailors of London set men's clothing styles. Many of their high-priced, copyrighted originals are then sold to dress manufacturers in America and other countries for mass production[5]

In recent years, it has become almost impossible to single out one style as the prevailing fashion. So many designs are available to the public at the same time that many different fashions exist simultaneously. A woman who owns an ankle-length skirt, a knee-length skirt, and jeans can be fashionable wearing any one of them.

5. *ibid*

Answer the following questions.

1.16   Define fashion. _____

_____

1.17   List the nine stages of a typical fashion cycle.

a. _____

b. _____

c. _____

d. _____

e. _____

f. _____

g. _____

h. _____

i. _____

1.18.   How has technology influenced the extent and duration of fashion cycles? _____

_____

1.19   How did Frances Hodgson Burnett's book, *Little Lord Fauntleroy* influence the style of boys' clothes? _____

1.20   What two changes took place in women's clothing styles during the World Wars?

a. _____ and b. _____

1.21 List and describe the three silhouettes that were the basis for fashion cycles.

a. _____

b. _____

c. _____

1.22 From where are the designers that have had the greatest influence on women's styles?

_____ Men's styles? _____

To gain a better understanding of fashions, their construction and their sales, study the three charts of terms and definitions that follow.

FASHION TERMS	DEFINITION
style	A particular design, shape, or type of apparel item. Examples: A-line skirt, Bermuda shorts, western shirts, crew-neck sweaters.
fashion	The display of the currently popular style of clothing, made popular through acceptance by a large segment of people.
apparel	Applies to all men's, women's, and children's clothing.
garment	Any article of apparel such as a dress, suit, coat; any particular clothing item.
silhouette	The shape of a clothing style; formed by width and length of the neckline, sleeves, waistline, and pants or skirt.
trend	The general direction that a fashion takes.
high fashion	Items that are the very latest or newest fashions, fine quality, and expensive.
avant-garde	Clothes that are the most daring and wild designs.
fad	A temporary, passing fashion; has great appeal to many people for a short period of time. Examples: accessories (bright colored sunglasses), particular fabrics and patterns, bell-bottom cords, tight fitting jeans.
craze	A passing love for a new creation, this has a display of emotion or crowd excitement with it.
classic	Item of clothing that continues to be popular despite fashion changes. Examples: white dress shirts, dark business suits, blue jeans, simple black dress.
wardrobe	All of the apparel a person owns; consists of all garments and accessories.

Complete the following activity.

1.23   Either draw or cut out and mount pictures of clothes that exemplify style, fad, and fashion in the boxes. Then describe why the clothes fit into the different categories.

a. Fad

This is an example of a fad because:

_____
_____
_____
_____
_____
_____
_____

b. Style

This is an example of a style because:

_____
_____
_____
_____
_____
_____
_____
_____

c. Fashion

This is an example of a fashion because:

_____
_____
_____
_____
_____
_____
_____
_____

Adult Check   _____

<u>Initial</u>   <u>Date</u>

CLOTHING CONSTRUCTION TERMS	DEFINITION
fit	Refers to how tight or loose a garment fits the person who is wearing it.
fitted garment	Is shaped to follow the lines of the body.
seam	The lines of stitches that join two garment pieces together.
darts	Short, tapered, stitched areas that enable the garment to fit the figure.
bodice	Area above the waist, such as upper part of a dress, usually closely fitted by a waistline seam.
draped garments	Those garments that are wrapped or hung loosely on the human body. Examples: Roman toga, Indian sari, ponchos, and draped skirts and gowns.
tailored garments	Made by first cutting garment pieces and then sewing them together to fit the shape of the body. Examples: jackets, pants, shirts.
composite garments	Made by combining tailored and draped methods. Examples: Japanese kimono, tunics, bathrobes, caftans, and capes.

Complete the following activity.

1.24 Either draw or cut out and mount pictures of draped, tailored, and composite clothes in the boxes. Then describe why the clothes fit into each category.

a. A draped garment

This is a draped garment because:

_____

_____

_____

_____

_____

_____

_____

b. A tailored garment

This is a tailored garment because:

_____

_____

_____

_____

_____

_____

_____

c. A composite garment

This is a composite garment because:

_____

_____

_____

_____

_____

_____

_____

_____

Adult Check

_____
Initial   Date

POINT TO PONDER

The *Hemline Index* is a theory that was developed by a research director of a stock brokerage firm. He noticed that when hemlines rose (1920s and again in the early 1960s), the stock market indexes also went up. When hemlines fell so did the stock markets (late 1920s and 1960s). Many feel this theory should not be taken seriously; even so, it reinforces the idea that peoples' moods are reflected in the way they dress.

CLOTHING BUSINESS TERMS	DEFINITION
haute couture	"Finest dressmaking" in French, came to mean high fashion industry referring to groups of firms, each with a designer.
couturier	Designer who often owns a firm.
custom-designed	A garment designed specifically for a particular person, having a special fit, design, and fabric for the person who ordered.
custom-made	Not designed for a particular person although it is made for that person, usually after seeing a sample garment, sketch, or picture.
copies	Looks like the original, made in quantity.
knock-offs	Lower-priced copies of garments, produced in great volume with lower quality materials and construction.
fashion piracy	The theft of design ideas or the use of a design without the consent of the originator.
ready to wear	Garments as in sizes 2–12; are those that are mass-produced in factories; manufactured in quantity according to sizes.
customers	People who buy and wear the garments.
retail stores	Sell to consumers, advertise, and sell items directly to the public.
wholesale business	Sells goods in large lots to retailers, distributing goods from large warehouses.
overruns	Extra clothes that were produced but weren't ordered for regular selling.
irregulars	Articles with slight imperfections.
seconds	Items that are soiled or have flaws.
promotions	Advertising efforts to improve sales.

Price markets are market categories based on retail selling prices of merchandise. There are basically three price markets in the apparel industry: high, moderate, and low. The high-priced market includes an extremely small number of people who buy fashionable clothing. They accept more unusual styles and colors than most people and are willing and able to spend more money. They also receive more publicity. Celebrities, royalty, and models would fall into this category.

The moderate-priced market includes garments that are factory produced in small numbers with dependable brand names and good fabrics. This makes up about one-third of all clothing sales. Upper- and upper-middle class professionals would make up the majority falling into this category.

The lower-priced market includes clothes mass produced in common styles, fabrics, and colors. This category is sold to the middle- and lower-class persons who make up the "mass market."

1.25   Explain the difference between a custom-designed garment and a custom-made garment.

_____

_____

_____

1.26   Describe the three price markets of the apparel industry._____

_____

_____

_____

1.27   Describe the influence of the *Hemline Index*._____

_____

_____

_____

:: **Match the following terms with their definitions.**

a. *avant-garde* clothes	b. back fullness silhouette	c. bell silhouette
d. bodice	e. classic	f. composite garment
g. couturier	h. custom-designed	i. custom-made
j. darts	k. draped garments	l. fashion leaders
m. fashion piracy	n. fitted	o. high fashion
p. irregulars	q. knock-offs	r. overruns
s. price markets	t. retail	u. seconds
v. style	w. tailored garments	x. tubular silhouette
y. wardrobe	z. wholesale	

1.28   _____   short, tapered, stitched areas that enable a garment to fit the figure

1.29   _____   the selling of merchandise directly to consumers

1.30   _____   a recurring style with extra fullness at the back only

1.31   _____   a designer who creates original, individually designed high fashions and usually owns the fashion house

1.32   _____   the selling of goods in large lots to retailers

1.33   _____   a particular design, shape or type of apparel item

1.34 _____ the apparel area above the waist, usually closely fitted

1.35 _____ articles of merchandise with slight imperfections that are sold to consumers at reduced prices

1.36 _____ all the garments and accessories a person owns

1.37 _____ daring, wild, and unconventional designs

1.38 _____ market categories based on retail selling prices of merchandise

1.39 _____ garments made by a combination of the tailored and draped methods

1.40 _____ trend-setting people who have enough status and credibility to introduce and popularize new styles

1.41 _____ a recurring style with fullness at the bottom

1.42 _____ the newest, most unique, and expensive apparel of fine quality and beautiful fabric, with limited acceptance

1.43 _____ apparel items that are wrapped or hung on the body and have characteristic folds of soft fabric

1.44 _____ a style that is slim and straight from top to bottom

1.45 _____ apparel made for the person who has ordered it, usually after seeing a sample garment, sketch, or picture

1.46 _____ extra first-quality items produced by a manufacturer but not ordered by retailers

1.47 _____ apparel items made by cutting garment pieces and then sewing them together to fit the shape of the body

1.48 _____ a garment or garment part that is shaped to follow the lines of the body

1.49 _____ clothing that stays popular though fashions change

1.50 _____ copies of other, usually higher-priced, garments

1.51 _____ items that are soiled or have noticeable flaws and must therefore be priced lower than perfect goods

1.52 _____ the theft of design ideas or the use of a design without the consent of the originator

1.53 _____ apparel created specifically for a particular person with special fit, design, and fabric

WARDROBE INVENTORY

People in industrialized nations often wear different types of clothing for different activities. In the course of a single week, a middle-class American youth may wear wool slacks and a sweater to class, a baseball uniform on the diamond, jeans and a sweatshirt while mowing the lawn, and a suit to a wedding. In less affluent countries, young people generally have only a couple of changes of clothing.

Choosing the right clothes and being a smart shopper takes time and effort. How have you done with creating a wardrobe that is both **utilitarian** and stylish? Take the following chart to your closet and fill it out. Be honest, so that you will know how to better improve your wardrobe choices in the future.

You will need to identify how many garments and in what colors you have for each clothing category. Describe its condition (needs mending or laundering). Explain why you do or do not like this item (maybe it doesn't fit, it's inappropriate, beyond repair). You can usually tell how you like a garment by how often you wear it. You may even include where you wear this item (shopping, school, work, exercise). The last item is to determine what you should do with the article; keep it, mend it, wash it, get rid of it, etc. Maybe you need more of this type of garment to round out your wardrobe. Be as detailed in this survey as possible; after all, it is for your personal benefit to help you improve your present wardrobe.

 Complete the following activity.

1.54   Complete the wardrobe inventory.

Clothes I have	Description	Condition	How I like it	Action to take
Dresses				
Skirts				
Pants				
Jeans				

14

Clothes I have	Description	Condition	How I like it	Action to take
Suits				
Blazers				
Jackets				
Jeans				
Shorts				
Casual Shirts/T-shirts				
Sweaters/Sweatshirts				

Clothes I have	Description	Condition	How I like it	Action to take
Coats				
Shoes/Boots				
Athletic Attire				
Undergarments				
Socks				
Sleepwear				
Hats/Gloves				

Clothes I have	Description	Condition	How I like it	Action to take
Neckwear				
Belts/Purses				
Formalwear				
Other				
Other				
Other				

Adult Check _____
Initial   Date

 Review the material in this section in preparation for the Self Test. The Self Test will check your mastery of this particular section. The items missed on this Self Test will indicate specific areas where restudy is needed for mastery.

SELF TEST 1

True or *False*: **If a statement is true, write *true* in the blank. If a statement is false, change the underlined word or words to make the statement true. Write the correct answer in the blank.** (each answer, 3 points).

1.01 _____ <u>Decorative</u> clothing gives physical protection to the body.

1.02 _____ Sunglasses, hats, and fur garments are examples of <u>protective</u> apparel that have gained fashion status.

1.03 _____ Clothing items for body <u>protection</u> show how different cultures view beauty.

1.04 _____ <u>Dress codes</u> are outfits or articles of clothing that are alike and specific to everyone in a certain group of people.

1.05 _____ <u>Identification</u> is gained when clothing is able to give a person a higher rank in society, along with social acceptance and peer approval.

1.06 _____ Different people have different <u>values</u>, such as thinking that comfort, economy, easy care, prestige, or the latest fashion look is important.

1.07 _____ The values and attitudes that influence a person's clothing choices <u>change</u> as that person goes through life.

1.08 _____ The <u>style</u> of a garment is shown by its design or shape.

1.09 _____ Avant-garde clothes are <u>widely popular</u>.

1.010 _____ <u>Consumers</u> acquire, use, and eventually discard clothing items.

1.011 _____ For our broad lifestyles today, <u>more</u> styles are popular at a time.

Match the terms (each answer, 2 points).

1.012 _____ the providing of physical safeguards

1.013 _____ a quality that gives pleasure to the senses and creates a positive emotional reaction in the viewer

1.014 _____ process of establishing or describing who or what someone is or what someone does

1.015 _____ written or unwritten rules of what should or should not be worn by a group of people

1.016 _____ the covering of a person's body according to the code of decency of that person's society

1.017 _____ act of obeying or agreeing with some given standard or authority

1.018 _____ an idea, belief, or thing that is important to a person

1.019 _____ rotal characteristics that distinguish an individual, especially his or her behavioral or emotional tendencies

1.020 _____ a person's feelings about or reactions to people, things, or ideas as formed from the person's values

1.021 _____ one's position or rank in comparison to others

a. identification

b. status

c. modesty

d. attitudes

e. beauty

f. personality

g. conformity

h. protection

i. values

j. dress code

18

Multiple choice. Write the correct letter on the blank (each answer, 2 points).

1.022 Clothing that gives protection from environmental dangers includes _____ .
    a. shoes, sterile gloves and masks, and grass skirts
    b. beaded necklaces and feathered hats
    c. clergy robes, wedding gowns, and graduation caps and gowns
    d. camouflage suits, raincoats, and bulletproof vests

1.023 Adornment refers to _____ .
    a. safety and security
    b. peer group pressure and personality
    c. dress codes and individuality
    d. decoration and beauty

1.024 Status is gained through clothing with _____ .
    a. service stripes or badges on uniforms
    b. expensive fabrics or jewelry
    c. the pelts of an ancient hunter's prey
    d. all of the above

1.025 Individuality is _____ .
    a. the force that makes people want to be like their friends
    b. usually a result of advertising and the availability of items
    c. self-expression that distinguishes one person from another
    d. the desire to look like the other individuals at school or work

1.026 A fashion trend is _____ .
    a. one of the parts that make up a complete garment
    b. a fine quality, expensive, high style item
    c. the direction in which fashion is moving
    d. the latest daring and wild fashion silhouette

1.027 Darts are put into garments to _____ .
    a. join two pieces of a garment together
    b. enable a garment to fit the figure
    c. make sure a garments length is correct
    d. all of the above

1.028 Composite garments are constructed _____ .
    a. by a combination of the tailored and draped methods
    b. with more than one type of fabric
    c. with two or more textures and colors
    d. with separate bodice and lower sections

1.029 Haute couture refers to _____ .
    a. the French high fashion industry
    b. fashion houses whose designers create original fashions
    c. expensive fashions made of luxury fabrics and in limited numbers
    d. all of the above

1.030 Knock-offs are _____ .
   a. jackets or sweaters that can be worn with several different garments
   b. lower priced garment copies produced in volume
   c. garments made specifically for a particular person
   d. marked-down items that are soiled or have flaws

1.031 Some experts feel the rise and fall of the hemline is related to _____ .
   a. the weather
   b. the stock market
   c. the amount of fabric available
   d. all of the above

Matching (each answer, 2 points).

1.032 _____ garments that are shaped to follow the lines of the body

1.033 _____ includes all the garments and accessories a person owns

1.034 _____ examples include suits, pants, and fitted jackets

1.035 _____ temporary, passing fashion or item that has great appeal to many people for a short period of time, then dies out quickly

1.036 _____ the display of the currently popular design of clothing

1.037 _____ any or all men's, women's and children's clothing

1.038 _____ has a slim skirt all around and mostly vertical lines

1.039 _____ an item of clothing that continues to be popular even when fashions change

a. tubular silhouette

b. fashion

c. classic

d. wardrobe

e. fad

f. fitted garments

g. tailored garments

h. apparel

Score _____

Adult Check _____

Initial   Date

II. DESIGN AND APPEARANCE

Clothing design is a visual art that deals with three-dimensional forms. It is a specialized, competitive, and often glamorous field. The designer must be able to create clothing that is both fashionable and functional. The finished garment has to fit the body of the wearer, be suitable for certain activities, and be relatively durable.

Every artist has had to apply the basic principles and elements of design to achieve the desired artistic effect. This section will help you to become confident in the use of these elements and principles and to follow them as you create that perfect individual fashion effect.

The next step is to learn how to use art principles in relation to the individual needs of your figure. An understanding of the styles and parts of a garment will help you to develop a wardrobe that will compliment your individual physical characteristics.

SECTION OBJECTIVES

Review these objectives. When you have completed this section, you should be able to:

5. Gain an understanding of the elements and principles of design.

6. Identify different garment styles.

7. Identify your body type for making proper clothing choices.

PRINCIPLES AND ELEMENTS OF DESIGN

Every fashion idea must be backed up with an understanding of color, print, texture, line, proportion, and balance. Fabric (color, print, and texture) is transformed into a design (line, proportion and balance). *For more information on this topic, see the LIFEPAC Art Elective course.*

Typically, the first thing we notice about a garment is its color. We talk about "the guy in the brown suit" or "the girl in the blue dress." Therefore, the fashion-conscious must be aware of the terms and principles of color.

The Terminology of Color. *Hue* (often used interchangeably with color) is the quality or characteristic by which we distinguish one color from another. The *primary hues* (red, yellow, blue) are the basic building blocks of color from which all others are blended. The *secondary hues* (orange, green, purple) are produced by mixing two primaries together. The *tertiary hues*, often called

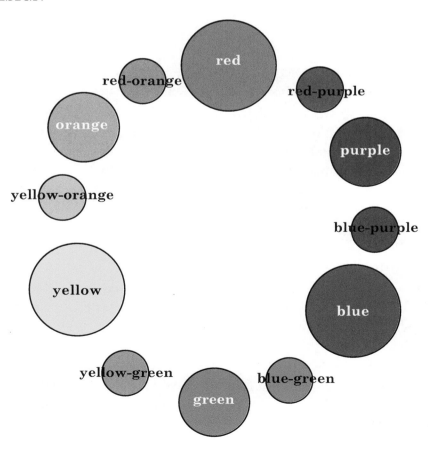

21

intermediates, stem from a combination of one primary and adjacent secondary together; they are the "double name" colors such as yellow-green and blue-violet. Note the primary hue is named first.

Value is the lightness or darkness of a color. Hues with white added are called *tints* and are higher in value than the original colors. Hues with black added are called *shades* and are correspondingly lower in value. Black, white, and gray are neutral colors.

Intensity is a color's brightness or dullness. *Tones* are hues with either their complementary color or gray added, reducing their intensity.

Color schemes are plans to utilize color for specific purposes. A *monochromatic* color scheme uses variations of one color or one color with black and white. Monochromatic is easy to achieve but can result in monotony if the variations are too similar. Add contrast by using extremes, such as beige against chocolate brown. *Analogous* color schemes use hues which are closely related on the color wheel, containing similar components (e.g., blue, blue-green, and green). Analogous schemes really help in developing mood and are often the most pleasing combinations. *Complementary* color schemes involve direct opposites on the color wheel, such as red and green or blue and orange. These are extremely bold. Variations of value and intensity should be used. Remember, colors are not isolated entities but work in relation to each other.

Color greatly affects the other elements in clothing design. When placed against each other, two colors with different values create a clear line. For example, a designer who wants to call attention to the lines of a navy-blue blazer might trim the lapels in white. Two colors of intensely opposite hues can produce an unpleasant visual "vibration," thus it would be difficult to focus on a the pattern of a fabric made of pink and chartreuse.

Colors also affect the appearance of the wearer's complexion. Magenta worn close to the face might make the skin appear greenish, while blue-green might give it a rosy cast. Colors and clothing styles go in and out of fashion. However, there is usually enough variety in fashionable colors to allow almost everyone a color that flatters.

Texture is both the look and feel of a fabric. Fabrics are rated by a nearly infinite number of qualities. For example, a fabric can be crisp, limp, heavy, light, nubby, smooth, dull, or shiny. Texture determines a garment's resistance to wear, ability to hold its shape, and amount of light it will reflect. Many textures may be used in a single costume. Compatible textures are determined by prevailing fashions.

Line is often **synonymous** with *style*. Every design is a carefully conceived structure of lines and shapes. Final garments present three major sets of lines: body (body shape), silhouette (dress shape), and detail lines (individual parts of the dress). Line is created in a variety of ways. The use of a patterned fabric, contrasting trim, or color values all serve to define lines. Some popular modern dresses use both trim and color to create horizontal and vertical lines. A clothing article's length, fullness, and cut are also important in determining line.

All elements in clothing design are strongly interrelated. Designing clothing requires a knowledge of all of these elements and the ability to use them effectively to create proportion, balance, emphasis, and rhythm: the principles of design.

Beautiful clothing is made to harmonize with the natural proportions of the body. *Proportion* is the spatial or size relationships of all the parts to one another and to the whole garment. All parts are related to one another in size, length, and bulk. Areas of identical size or divisions of space such as halves, fourths, or thirds used together can be dull. For a more interesting effect, use relationships in terms of one to three, three to five, and so on. *Scale* also refers to size relationships, describing how large or small elements are.

Balance is equilibrium in the distribution of the weight of the design elements. It is achieved by maintaining equal amounts of interest in either direction from the natural center of interest. *Formal balance* is when the design elements on either side of the center of interest are equal or exactly alike; it is symmetrical. *Informal balance* is when the design elements on either side of the center of interest are not identical; it is asymmetrical. This is accomplished by shifting the center of interest with emphasis. *Emphasis* attracts the eye to one feature or area and **subordinates** the others. It can be created with color, texture, line-trimming shapes, tucks, gathers, buttons, etc.

Rhythm is created by the eye moving smoothly and easily, connecting points of interest without jerking from point to point. It can be created by repetition, **gradation**, **transition**, **opposition**, and **radial arrangement** of lines, shapes, colors, and textures.

Answer the following questions.

2.1   Define *hue*._____

2.2   The basic building blocks of color are known as _____ . They are _____ , _____ and _____ .

2.3   Secondary hues are produced by mixing two _____ together. The secondary hues are _____ , _____ , and _____ .

2.4   How are tertiary hues made? _____

2.5   Give an example of tertiary color. _____

2.6   The lightness or darkness of a color is known as the _____ of that color.

2.7   What is the difference between a tint and a shade? _____

_____

2.8   Black, white and gray are examples of _____ colors.

2.9   What is the relationship between intensity and tone?_____

_____

2.10 List and describe the three color schemes given in your text. _____

_____

_____

2.11 Color can affect the element of _____ when two colors of intensely opposite hues are placed next to each other.

2.12 _____ refers to both the look and feel of a fabric.

2.13 What are the three major lines present in final garments?_____

_____

2.14 _____ applies to the spatial or size relationships of all the parts to one another and to the whole garment.

2.15 _____ attracts the eye to one feature or area and subordinates the others.

2.16 _____ is the flow of the eyes from left to right, connecting points of interest smoothly and easily.

2.17 Define *gradation*. _____

Answer *true* **or** *false*.

2.18 _____ You should use only one texture in a single costume.

2.19 _____ It is best to use divisions of halves, fourths and thirds together to achieve good proportion.

2.20 _____ Scale describes how large or small the elements of the garment are.

2.21 _____ Formal balance is also referred to as asymmetrical.

GARMENT STYLES AND PARTS

It is important to choose clothes that compliment your body type. Some garments look better on one person than on another. Because everyone is proportioned differently, it is important to have a working knowledge of the parts that make up the garments and the different styles of these parts. This way you can select the styles that complement your body the best.

The following fashion terminology has been categorized into garment parts. It includes terms commonly used to describe silhouettes, styles, and details of clothing design. A knowledgeable and conversational use of the words listed here will certainly increase your fashion confidence.

DRESS SILHOUETTE

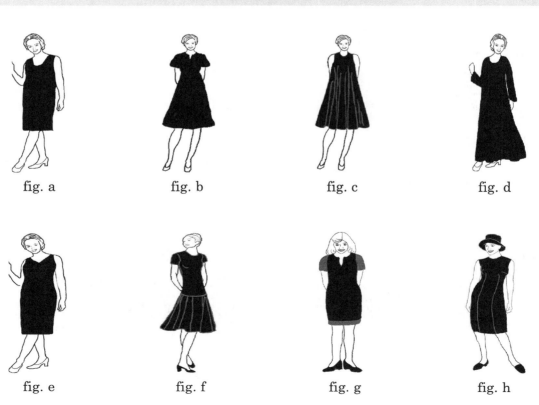

fig. a   fig. b   fig. c   fig. d

fig. e   fig. f   fig. g   fig. h

24

fig. i

fig. j

fig. k

fig. l

DRESS SILHOUETTE

Refer to images listed above.

Shift	fig. a	Loose-fitting dress.
A-line	fig. b	Dress or skirt resembling shape of an A.
Tent	fig. c	Large, billowing dress that hangs loose from the shoulders.
Empire	fig. d	Dress style that has a high waistline seam.
Sheath/Chemise	fig. e	Dress that hangs from the shoulder and has inward shaping at the waist, but no waistline seam.
Low-waist	fig. f	Dress with a long torso or lowered waistline.
Tunic	fig. g	Long top, worn over another garment.
Princess	fig. h	Fitted dress style with seam lines going up and down the entire length and no horizontal waistline seam.
Blouson	fig. i	Dress style with blousy fullness in the top, usually with a fitted skirt or a belt.
Shirtwaist	fig. j	Similar to a sheath, but front-button closure entire length of dress.
Coat dress	fig. k	Dress with coat-like lines and front closure.
Jumper	fig. l	One-piece sleeveless dress with a complete or partial bodice usually worn over a blouse.

SKIRT STYLE

fig. a

fig. b

fig. c

fig. d

fig. e

fig. f

fig. g

fig. h

SKIRT STYLE	Refer to images listed above.	
Straight	fig. a	Slim silhouette and no added fullness.
Gathered	fig. b	Fullness is created by fabric being pulled together at the waist without structured folds.
Wrap-around	fig. c	Fabric wraps around the body and overlaps at a full-length opening.
Gored (4 gore, 6 gore)	fig. d	Has panels formed by vertical seam lines.
Full	fig. e	Skirt that has pleats or gathers.
Pleated (knife, single front, double front)	fig. f	Structured folds of cloth that gives fullness in a garment.
Dirndl	fig. g	Gathered only slightly.
Circular	fig. h	A very full skirt that forms a circle when laid flat.

PANTS/SLACKS/TROUSERS

fig. a

fig. b

fig. c

fig. d

fig. e   fig. f   fig. g   fig. h

fig. i   fig. j   fig. k   fig. l

PANTS/SLACKS/TROUSERS

Refer to images listed above and on previous page.

Straight	fig. a	A pant with a slim silhouette and no added fullness.
Tapered	fig. b	Legs of pants are narrower at the hem than at the knee.
Flared	fig. c	Legs of pants become wider near the bottom.
Palazzo	fig. d	Flared from the waistline and very full at the bottom.
Harem	fig. e	Flared pants that are gathered at the ankle.
Jumpsuit	fig. f	A garment with a bottom (pants) attached to the top (bodice).
Hip-huggers	fig. g	Pants that are belted or fastened at the hips rather than at the waist.
Jeans	fig. h	Pants made of a stout twill cotton fabric.
Knickers	fig. i.	Loose-fitting short pants, gathered in at the knee.
Gauchos	fig. j	Pants that end just below the knee with legs like wide tubes.
Culottes	fig. k	A woman's casual trouser, cut full to resemble a skirt.
Shorts (bermuda, shorts, boys shorts)	fig. l	Legs of pants cut above the knee.

fig. a   fig. b   fig. c   fig. d

fig. e   fig. f   fig. g   fig. h

fig. i   fig. j

SLEEVE STYLE Refer to images listed above.

Sleeveless	fig. a	A garment designed with no sleeves.
Set-in (short, three-quarter, long, cuff)	fig. b	Sleeves that are set into the armhole of the garment.
Raglan	fig. c	A sleeve style with a shaped seam in the garment originating from the underarm.
Kimono	fig. d	Sleeves are continuous extensions out from the garment.
Cap	fig. e	A very short sleeve just covering the shoulder, sometimes called a French sleeve.
Batwing	fig. f	A kimono style sleeve that is very low and loose at the underarm.
Dropped shoulder	fig. g	A sleeve style that has a horizontal seam going around the upper part of the arm.
Peasant	fig. h	Full sleeve set into dropped shoulder and usually gathered into wrist-line.
Bell sleeve	fig. i	Full sleeve, flaring at the lower edge like a bell.
Dolman	fig. j	A woman's mantle with cape-like arm pieces instead of sleeves.

fig. a

fig. b

fig. c

fig. d

fig. e

fig. f

fig. g

fig. h

fig. i

fig. j

NECKLINE STYLE		Refer to images listed above.
Jewel	fig. a	Simple, round neckline at base of neck.
Scoop	fig. b	A neckline that is lowered and rounded in front.
U-neck	fig. c	U-shaped in front. Also known as the horseshoe neckline.
V-neck	fig. d	V-shaped in front.
Bateau	fig. e	Follows the curve of the collarbone. Also known as the boat neckline.
Cowl	fig. f	A neckline that is draped with flowing folds.
Décolleté	fig. g	A low-necked garment, exposing neck and/or back or cleavage of bosom as in formal evening dress.
Keyhole	fig. h	Round neckline with inverted wedge-shaped opening at front.
Crew	fig. i.	Round neckline that hugs the throat.
Halter	fig. j	Neckline having band around neck, attached to front of a backless bodice.

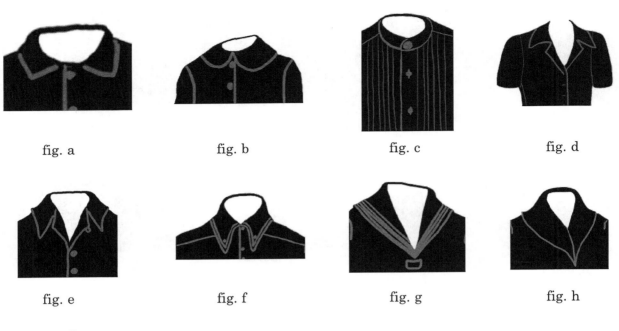

fig. a   fig. b   fig. c   fig. d

fig. e   fig. f   fig. g   fig. h

fig. i

COLLAR STYLE		Refer to images listed above.
Pointed flat	fig. a	A close-fitting flat collar with pointed corners and rounded neckline.
Peter Pan	fig. b	A close-fitting flat collar with rounded corners and rounded neckline.
Mandarin	fig. c	Small standing collar that hugs the neck.
Rolled	fig. d	First stands up from the neck edge, then falls down to rest on the garment.
Convertible	fig. e	A rolled collar style that can be worn closed or open to form a V shape with a lapel.
Buttondown	fig. f	A convertible style collar with buttons on the pointed-corners that can be buttoned to the front of the shirt. (example) Oxford shirt.
Middy sailor	fig. g	Type of slip-on blouse with a sailor collar. Sailor collar is a rolled collar that has a large square section in the back of the garment.
Chelsea	fig. h	A very deep v-neckline with rolled collar. Also known as a shawl collar.
Turtleneck	fig. i	A high rolled collar that hugs the throat.

COAT STYLES

fig. a

fig. b

fig. c

fig. d

COAT STYLE   Refer to images listed above.

Coat	fig. a	A warm or weatherproof garment that is worn over regular clothing.
Trench	fig. b	A waterproof, usually double-breasted, belted overcoat, with large pockets and straps on the shoulders and lower sleeves.
Chesterfield	fig. c	A single-breasted overcoat with a velvet collar.
Polo	fig. d	A double-breasted, often belted overcoat made of camel's hair or similar fabric.

JACKET STYLES

fig. a

fig. b

fig. c

fig. d

fig. e

fig. f

fig. g

fig. h

fig. i

fig. j

fig. k

fig. l

fig. m

JACKET STYLE		Refer to images listed above and on previous page.
Jacket	fig. a	A short coat.
Parka	fig. b	A heavy winter jacket with a hood.
Blazer	fig. c	A classic jacket or sport coat.
Windbreaker	fig. d	A waist-length or slightly longer, lightweight, wind-resistant jacket, often having a collar, for sports or other outdoor wear.
Pea	fig. e	A sailor's double-breasted jacket of thick navy blue wool.
Bolero	fig. f	Short jacket that ends above the waist, Spanish origin.
Pullover	fig. g	Slips over the head when put on or taken off.
Cardigan	fig. h	Close-fitting collarless jacket, sweater or bodice with center front closing.
Single-breasted jacket	fig. i	Held shut with one row of buttons.
Double-breasted jacket	fig. j	Has a wider overlap and two rows of buttons.
Vest	fig. k	A sleeveless, close-fitting, jacket-like garment that covers the chest and back.
Cape	fig. l	A cloak that hangs from the neck and shoulders and has no sleeves.
Poncho	fig. m	An unshaped, blanket-like outer garment with a slit or hole in the middle so it can be slipped over the head.

fig. a   fig. b   fig. c   fig. d

fig. e   fig. f   fig. g   fig. h

fig. i   fig. j   fig. k

MISCELLANEOUS GARMENT PARTS AND ACCESSORIES	Refer to images listed above.	
Lapels	fig. a	A part of a garment folded back on the breast, usually as a continuation of a coat collar.
Pocket	fig. b	A built-in "envelope" in a garment to hold things.
Tab	fig. c	A decorative fabric piece that goes out from the edge of a pocket.
Hood	fig. d	Head covering that is attached at the neckline of a garment.
Waistband	fig. e	A band of fabric that fastens together at the waistline of pants or skirt.
Yoke	fig. f	A band or shaped piece, usually at the shoulder or hips, to give shape and support to the garment below it.
Flaps	fig. g	Decorative fabric pieces that fall down over the openings of pockets.

Ascot	fig. h	A broad scarf worn at the neck like a necktie.
Cravat	fig. i	Necktie folded or tied at front with ends tucked inside garment.
Dickey	fig. j	Detachable shirt front.
Jabot	fig. k	Ruffle worn down front of bodice and fastened at neck.

Complete the crossword puzzle.

2.22

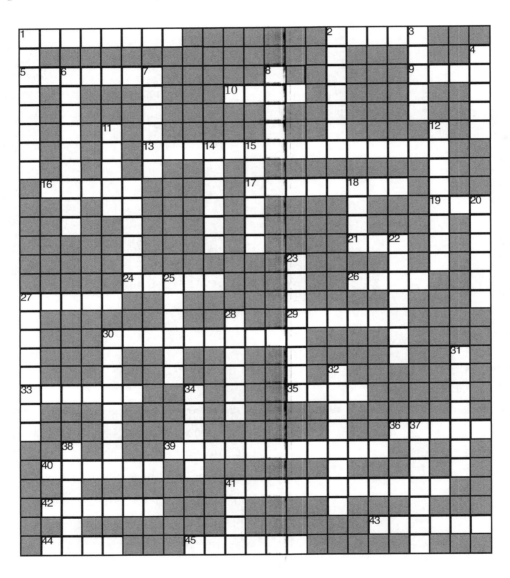

ACROSS

1. close-fitting collarless jacket, sweater, or bodice with center front closing

2. a heavy winter jacket with a hood

5. a low-waist dress that has a long torso or _____ waistline

9. a cloak that hangs from the neck and shoulders and has no sleeves

10. head covering that is attached at the neck-line of a garment

13. a sleeve style that has a horizontal seam going around the upper part of the arm (two words)

16. flared pants that are gathered at the ankle

FAMILY AND CONSUMER SCIENCE

four

LIFEPAC TEST

81/101

Name_____

Date_____

Score_____

FAMILY AND CONSUMER SCIENCE 04: LIFEPAC TEST

Matching (each answer, 2 points).

1. _____ synthetic fiber
2. _____ enables the garment to fit the figure
3. _____ high fashion industry
4. _____ lower priced copies of garments
5. _____ part of the garment above the waist
6. _____ an idea, belief or thing that is important to a person
7. _____ total characteristics that distinguish an individual, especially his or her behavior or emotional tendencies
8. _____ an individual's reaction to people, things or ideas
9. _____ structured folds of cloth
10. _____ standing collar
11. _____ a neckline that is draped with flowing folds
12. _____ Spanish styled short jacket
13. _____ flat collar
14. _____ panels formed by vertical seams
15. _____ fitted dress style with seam lines going up and down entire length
16. _____ dress style with high waistline
17. _____ follows the curve of the collarbone

a. attitude
b. bateau
c. bodice
d. bolero
e. cowl
f. dart
g. gored
h. Empire
i. haute couture
j. knock-offs
k. mandarin
l. nylon
m. personality
n. Peter Pan
o. pleated
p. princess
q. value

Fill in the blank (each answer, 2 points).

18. If you are tall, you should wear _____ .
    a. horizontal lines or stripes
    b. straight skirts
    c. a one color effect from head to foot
    d. all of the above

19. If you are plump, you should wear _____ .
    a. horizontal contrasts
    b. longer skirt hemlines
    c. fuller skirts
    d. all of the above

20. A jacket is a good example of a _____ .
    a. draped garment
    b. composite garment
    c. tailored garment
    d. proportioned garment

21. The display of the currently popular style of clothing is a _____ .
    a. fad
    b. fashion
    c. trend
    d. style

1

22. Clothing that reflects concern for others in society should be _____ .
   a. modest
   b. "softening" in line for girls
   c. masculine in appearance for boys
   d. all of the above

23. The term referring to the name of a color is: _____ .
   a. hue
   b. value
   c. shade
   d. intensity

24. The color scheme that uses colors opposite on the color wheel is called _____ .
   a. monochromatic
   b. analogous
   c. complimentary

25. Sort clothes for washing by _____ .
   a. color and fabric
   b. bulk and amount of soil
   c. none of the above
   d. both a and b

26. A tape measure should be _____ .
   a. 60" long
   b. 54" long
   c. 5' long
   d. both a and c

27. _____ is good for the removal of a non-washable ink stain.
   a. petroleum jelly
   b. milk
   c. cold water
   d. none of the above

28. Pinking shears are used for _____ .
   a. clipping, snipping and trimming
   b. cutting seams open
   c. finishing seams and raw edges
   d. removing stitches

Matching. Words may be used more than once and there may be more than one answer for each question (each answer, 2 points).

29. _____ natural fiber that draws heat from the body   a. cotton

30. _____ generic name of a man-made fiber   b. linen

31. _____ fleece of sheep   c. silk

32. _____ synthesized fiber   d. wool

33. _____ natural fiber that does not dye easily   e. polyester

34. _____ needs moth proofing   f. Orlon

35. _____ from the flax plant   g. acrylic

36. _____ trademark name

37. _____ natural fiber that is less apt to wrinkle

38. _____ requires no dry cleaning

2

Answer *true* **or** *false* (each answer, 1 point).

39. _____ Zippers should be closed before the garment is laundered.

40. _____ Whites are washed with light colored garments.

41. _____ Milk is good for removal of non-washable ink stains.

42. _____ Snaps are used on openings with little or no strain.

43. _____ Synthesized means made from cellulose.

44. _____ Status is gained when clothing is able to give a person a higher rank in society, along with social acceptance and peer approval.

45. _____ The word apparel applies to all men's, women's and children's clothing.

46. _____ Man-made fibers were first experimented with in the 20th the century.

47. _____ Rayon is an example of a man-made natural fiber.

48. _____ Synthetics wrinkle easily.

49. _____ Safety pins should be used for emergency repairs only.

50. _____ A pocket seam is an example of a stress seam.

51. _____ The best hand stitch for mending a ripped seam is the staystitch.

52. _____ A good hand stitch for mending a hem with an overcast edge is the blindstitch.

53. _____ The shank button sits on top of the buttonhole.

Matching (each answer, 2 points).

54. _____ tint

55. _____ dull colors

56. _____ warm colors

57. _____ horizontal lines

58. _____ bulky fabrics

a. increases your size

b. decreases your size

17. slips over the head when put on or taken off

19. a very short sleeve just covering the shoulder

21. a decorative fabric piece that goes out from the edge of a pocket

24. a ruffle worn down the front of a bodice

26. head covering that is attached at the neckline of a garment

27. type of slip-on blouse with a sailor collar

29. structured folds of cloth that give fullness in a garment

30. a garment designed with no sleeves

33. a sleeve style with a shaped seam in the garment originating from the underarm

35. large billowing dress that hangs loose from the shoulders

36. a neckline that is lowered and rounded in front

39. a waist-length or slightly longer, light-weight, wind-resistant jacket

40. a _____ garment is shaped to follow the lines of the body

41. a rolled collar style that can be worn closed or open

42. short jacket that ends above the waist, Spanish origin

43. dress that hangs from the shoulder and has inward shaping at the waist, but no waistline seam

44. a band or shaped piece, usually at the shoulders or hips

45. neckline having a band around the neck, attached to front of a backless bodice

DOWN

1. a woman's casual trouser

2. pants that are flared from the waistline and very full at the bottom

3. a broad scarf worn at the neck like a necktie

4. pants made of stout twill cotton fabric

6. a band of fabric that fastens together at the waistline of pants or skirts

7. skirt that is gathered only slightly

8. skirt that has panels formed by vertical seam lines

11. simple round neckline at base of neck

12. fitted dress style with seam lines going up and down the entire length and no horizontal waistline seam

14. an unshaped blanket-like outer garment

15. dress style that has a high waistline

18. a sleeveless, close-fitting, jacket-like garment that covers the chest and back

20. a built-in "envelope" in a garment to hold things

22. dress style with blousy fullness in the top, usually with a fitted skirt or a belt

23. a garment with a bottom attached to the top

25. follows the curve of the collarbone

27. small standing collar that hugs the neck

28. a classic jacket or sport coat

30. a pant with a slim silhouette and no added fullness

31. round neckline with inverted wedge-shaped opening at front

32. loose-fitting short pants gathered at the knee

34. long top, worn over another garment

37. a very deep v-neckline with rolled collar

38. sleeves that are continuous extensions out from the garment

41. a neckline that is draped with flowing folds

CLOTHES FOR YOU

We have studied the principles and elements of design which have an important role in the overall visual impact of clothing. As important as a working knowledge of garment styles and parts are, there are several other areas to consider to put together an attractive complete look.

The most important thing is to relate everything to you. Don't forget that you have proportions of your own. A garment that looks perfectly proportioned with good line, color, and texture on the hanger may not look so great on you. The next step is to learn how to use art principles in relation to the individual needs of your figure.

Height is the most important factor when trying to cover a figure problem or when trying to emphasize a particularly positive feature. The following paragraphs will describe the important principles that the short woman, 5' 4" and under and the tall woman, 5' 7" and over, should follow when selecting garments. If you fall somewhere between, study yourself and decide where your bone structure places you and the impression of desired height you wish to convey.

Gentlemen: although most of the following information is directed primarily to the ladies, you will be able to glean some of the basic principles for a well-balanced and proportioned appearance. Don't skip this section.

Short. A short person should avoid very large prints; they will be greatly out of scale with your build and the size of your garment, giving an appearance of being shorter and wider. You should avoid the unnecessary bulk of billowing skirts and loose-fitting front-pleat pants or very heavy fabrics. Short fitted jackets, gently flared silhouettes, and delicate detailing are your best choices. The scale of your accessories should be appropriate as well; heavy jewelry or handbags (briefcases) can completely destroy your efforts.

Line is also important. If you want to add inches to your height, no matter what your weight, depend on the illusions the vertical line can give you. The princess style of dress will give a strong impression of height. V-necklines, pleats, raised or lowered waistlines will all tend to heighten your appearance. Anything that cuts your overall appearance in half like belts, tight waists, very short skirts or shorts, or repeated horizontal construction will tend to shorten your appearance.

If you are short and weight is also a factor, a little more effort is required. Once again the vertical lines are the best way to slenderize your appearance. Avoid gathers or pleats unless they are stitched down to the hip. Wear simple lines.

Color should be of great consideration. Monochromatic garments will help elongate your appearance. Warm colors and bright colors will tend to increase your stature visibly. If you are slim, you can almost wear any color you want. Solid colors, neat textures, and small prints are best for your body build. If you are slightly heavy, avoid vivid colors and shiny fabrics except when used as accent.

Tall. If you are tall, you have a great advantage. You may wear bright colors, exotic prints, and dramatic lines. However, you will need to select clothes that are right for your size. Very tiny prints on a tall, large person will emphasize the contrast between their delicacy and the size of the person wearing them. You can select colorful prints, nubby fabrics, and bold stripes. Find the balance for your height with horizontal lines. Wide belts, medium-long jackets, and crosswise stripes are good choices.

Line, too, affects the tall. If you are tall and willowy, the world of fashion is open to you. Be creative. If you have a full figure, lean toward easy fitting, non-fussy silhouettes and curved or diagonal vertical lines. Gently lowered necklines with ties or collars will emphasize the face while balancing a heavier figure. Orderly prints will be better looking than splashy plaids or repeated horizontal stripes. If you are extremely tall and thin and you wish to appear shorter, wear a wide colorful cummerbund, crosswise yokes, and other horizontal construction lines.

Color can also be used to your advantage. Make your color selection according to your weight. Cool colors as well as the dull hues make the figure appear smaller. To appear more slender, wear medium to dark color values in your solids and soft shades for prints, plaids, and textures. To add bulk and roundness to the slim figure, select bright colors with shiny or chunky textures. Contrasting separates are recommended if you are tall because they cut your height and therefore balance your appearance.

In addition to the basic concept of height, your individual physical characteristics should be considered as well. Shoulder width, chest or bust size, width of hips, length of waist, etc., are all areas of concern when selecting clothing that will compliment your appearance. Camouflage can be accomplished with careful use of color, print, line, or texture. Well-placed lines in the form of trim or accessories can draw attention to figure pluses or away from negative features. Soft, filmy, clingy fabrics are slenderizing to the silhouette. Because clingy fabrics hug the body, they reveal figure irregularities. Lightweight fabrics with a little more firmness will slenderize the body and help hide figure problems.

You can shift emphasis and give an illusion of weight or size by using: a print in opposition to a solid, detail to simplicity, a bright color to dull one, heavily textured fabric to a light flat fabric, shiny to dull finish. "Each design element does not work by itself but interacts and relates to the others to create the whole."[1]

The following chart should help you create the illusion of that "perfect" figure for yourself. [2]

FIGURE DEFINITION	COLOR CHOICE	LINE CHOICE	TEXTURE CHOICE
Tall, thin	multi-colored outfits, light colors	horizontal lines, double-breasted closing, horizontal lines below waistline	almost any type, large weaves, plush textures
Tall, heavy	grayed hues, medium values	curved or diagonal lines, loosely fitted blouses, slightly flared shirts, V-neck	plain fabric
Short, thin	warm, bright, use close values, one-color outfits	vertical lines, small scale prints and plaids	Crisp but not heavy, soft, smooth, shiny finishes
Short, heavy	one-color scheme, dark values	vertical lines	dull textures, smooth surface, small prints
Heavy hips	light bodice, dark skirt	Y-necklines, slightly flared skirts, tent styles	smooth, firm fabrics
Large bust	dark colors for bodice; light, bright colors for skirt	pointed collars, simple necklines, long sleeves	medium to light weight
Small bust	light, bright colors	horizontal stripes, large collars, interesting necklines, jackets and vests	Medium and heavy weights, napped or bulky

---

[1]Much of the material about design elements and choosing clothes that flatter the figure were taken from *The New Vogue Sewing Book.*

[2]This chart was taken from *Family and Consumer Science LIFEPAC 6,* 1979 ed.

Answer the following questions.

2.23 What is the most important factor to consider when trying to cover a figure problem or when trying to emphasize a positive feature? _____

2.24 If you are short, avoid _____ prints and _____ fabrics.

2.25 If you are short, wear clothes with _____ lines such as the _____ style of dress.

2.26 If you are short and weight is a factor, avoid _____ and _____ unless they are stitched down to the hip.

2.27 If you are tall, you will need to find the balance for your height with _____ lines.

2.28 If you are a tall, full-figured person, wear _____ or _____ lines.

2.29 How can you emphasize your face if you are a tall, full-figured person?_____

_____

2.30 Tall people should make their color selections according to their _____ .

Circle the correct answer(s).

2.31 (**Dark / Light**) colors tend to make the body appear small and (**dark / light**) colors tend to make you look larger.

2.32 (**Bright / Dull**) colors make you appear larger.

Answer *true* **or** *false*.

2.33 _____ Color-contrasting separates are recommended for the short person.

Complete the following activity.

2.34 Analyze your own figure assets and problems by completing the following chart.

My Personal Figure Analysis

A. **Your Body:** Check the following characteristics that apply to you.

Proportion:

_____	long neck	_____	average length waist
_____	short neck	_____	long legs
_____	average neck	_____	short legs
_____	long-waisted	_____	average length legs
_____	short-waisted	_____	tall
_____	short	_____	average height

Weight distribution:

_____ overweight	_____ wide hips
_____ average	_____ average hips
_____ underweight	_____ narrow hips
_____ thick waist	_____ heavy arms
_____ thin waist	_____ average arms
_____ average waist	_____ thin arms
_____ large bust/chest	_____ heavy legs
_____ average bust/chest	_____ average legs
_____ small bust/chest	_____ thin legs

Figure irregularities:

_____ tummy bulge

_____ over-waisted bulge

_____ prominent derrière

_____ swayback

_____ other, explain _____

_____

Coloring: _____ fair _____ olive _____ medium _____ tan _____ dark _____

B. **Weight and Proportion:** Review the answers you checked above. Decide which types of clothing you should choose and clothing that you should avoid for your particular figure. Refer to the garment styles and parts terms for ideas.

	CHOOSE	AVOID
Length of neck		
Length of waist		
Length of leg		
Height and weight		

C. **The Colors for You:**

1. What colors look best with your coloring? _____

   Why? _____

   What colors should you avoid? _____

   Why? _____

2. What colors are best for your body type? _____

   Why? _____

   Are there any you should avoid? _____ Which ones? _____

   Why? _____

D. **The Lines for You:**

1. Which line(s) should you wear? _____

   _____

   Why? _____

2. Which lines should you avoid? _____

   Why? _____

E. **The Textures for You:**

1. Which textures are most becoming? _____

   Why? _____

2. Which textures should you avoid? _____

   Why? _____

F. **The Scale for You:**

1. What size prints or patterns look best on you? _____

   Why? _____

2. Are there any that you should not wear? _____ Which ones? _____

   _____

   Why? _____

Adult Check _____
                          Initial   Date

Complete the following activity.

2.35 On a separate sheet of paper, design and draw your own garment (girls — dress, boys — blazer). Choose a silhouette style, sleeve style, and neckline or collar style with lines that flatter your figure. Color your garment in a color scheme that will flatter you. You will need a pencil, colored pencils, or crayons.

Adult Check _____
                          Initial   Date

Review the material in this section in preparation for the Self Test. The Self Test will check your mastery of this particular section. The items missed on this Self Test will indicate specific areas where restudy is needed for mastery.

SELF TEST 2

Choose the letter of the correct answer (each answer, 3 points).

2.01 _____ are the three primary colors.
    a. Red, yellow, blue   b. Green, orange, purple
    c. White, black, gray

2.02 A fad is _____ .
    a. the display of the currently popular design of clothing
    b. an item of clothing that continues to be popular even when fashions change
    c. a temporary, passing fashion that dies out quickly

2.03 _____ is term referring to the name of a color.
    a. Hue   b. Value
    c. Shade   d. Intensity

2.04 The color scheme that uses colors opposite each other on the color wheel is called _____ .
    a. monochromatic   b. analogous
    c. complementary

2.05 A dress style that hangs from the shoulder and has an inward shaping at the waist, but no waistline seam is a(n) _____ .
    a. empire   b. sheath
    c. princess   d. shirtwaist

2.06 A skirt that has structured folds of cloth to give it fullness is _____ .
    a. pleated   b. gathered
    c. dirndl   d. gored

2.07 Pants that are flared from the waist and very full at the bottom are _____ .
    a. harem   b. gauchos
    c. palazzo   d. tapered

2.08 A _____ sleeve is most like a kimono style sleeve.
    a. raglan   b. batwing
    c. dolman   d. peasant

2.09 Clothing serves a _____ function.
    a. protection   b. modesty
    c. status   d. adornment
    e. all of the above

2.010 A _____ neckline is also known as the boatneck.
    a. scoop   b. crew
    c. bateau   d. jewel

2.011 The _____ is a standing collar.
    a. mandarin   b. Peter Pan
    c. chelsea   d. convertible

2.012 A detachable shirt front is called a _____ .

    a. ascot   b. dickey

    c. cravat   d. jabot

2.013 Which of the following statements is NOT true for short people? _____

    a. They should avoid garments with very large prints.

    b. They should wear garments with vertical lines.

    c. They should wear a complementary color scheme.

    d. They should wear V-necklines.

2.014 A tall person should wear _____ .

    a. horizontal lines   b. small prints

    c. monochromatic colors   d. all of the above

2.015 Which of the following statements is true? _____

    a. *Little Lord Fauntleroy* introduced the velvet suit into fashion.

    b. The World Wars influenced fashion when easy-to-care-for and plain dresses were introduced.

    c. Kings and Queens had a great influence on style.

    d. all of the above

2.016 Gloria is tall and heavy. _____ are colors that will help her appear thinner.

    a. Cool colors   b. Bright colors

    c. Tints of colors   d. Primary colors

2.017 Pam would like a skirt from a receding color to make her hips appear smaller. She should choose _____ .

    a. yellow   b. red

    c. green   d. purple

Match the terms (each answer, 2 points).

2.018 _____ a neckline that is draped with flowing folds   a. parka

2.019 _____ a rolled collar style that can be worn closed or open   b. convertible

2.020 _____ loose-fitting short pants gathered at the waist   c. bolero

2.021 _____ close-fitting collarless jacket, sweater or bodice with a center front closing   d. jabot

                                                              e. cardigan

2.022 _____ a classic jacket or sports coat   f. cowl

2.023 _____ short jacket ending above the waist   g. blazer

2.024 _____ heavy winter jacket with a hood   h. blouson

2.025 _____ a single- or double-breasted topcoat with a narrow velvet collar   i. knickers

                                                              j. Chesterfield

2.026 _____ a ruffle worn down the front of a bodice

2.027 _____ a dress style with blousy fullness in the top, usually with a fitted skirt or a belt

Answer *true* **or** *false* (each answer, 2 points).

2.028 _____ Short people should avoid heavy fabrics.

2.029 _____ A princess style dress is a good choice for a tall person.

2.030 _____ You can give an illusion of weight or size by using a print in opposition to a solid.

2.031 _____ Soft, filmy, clingy fabrics are slenderizing to the silhouette.

2.032 _____ Light colors tend to make the body appear small.

2.033 _____ A tall, full-figured person should wear curved or diagonal vertical lines.

2.034 _____ Contrasting separates are recommended for the tall person.

2.035 _____ Intensity is the lightness and darkness of a hue.

2.036 _____ Curved lines give an appearance of femininity.

2.037 _____ Men's fashions are greatly influenced by the Bond Street Tailors of London.

Short answer (answer, 10 points).

2.038 Distinguish between a draped garment, a tailored garment, and a composite garment. Include examples of each.

_____

_____

_____

_____

_____

_____

III. TEXTILES AND FABRICS

Fibers are the basic components of textile fabrics. Each has its own unique characteristics that set it apart from the other fibers, making the fabrics created from it unique as well. There are four main steps in the production of fabrics. First, fiber production: raw materials are processed into various fibers. Second, yarn production: mills spin fibers into yarn. Third, fabric manufacturing: plants weave or knit yarns into fabric. Fourth, fabric finishing: finishing is done by bleaching, dying, printing, or applying special coatings.

The structure, weave, and finish of the fabric are strong indicators of its quality, but the original personality (fiber content) is still evident in the resulting fabric and is central to its use and care.

The primary distinction in fiber types is a very simple one—a fiber is either natural or man-made.

SECTION OBJECTIVE

Review this objective. When you have completed this section, you should be able to:

    8. Identify various types of both natural and man-made fabrics.

NATURAL FIBERS

Fibers exist in nature in a variety of **guises**. These natural fibers are found in both animals and plants: the wool of the sheep, the fine filament from which the silk worm spins his cocoon, the linen made from the fibrous stalk of the flax plant, cotton that grows as a puff protecting the seeds of the cotton plant. The very depth of their structure give these natural fibers their distinct characteristics: the familiar warmth of wool, the downy softness of cotton, the rich, dry texture of silk, and the crisp sheen of linen originate in the plant or animal that made them.

The following table will give you a comparison of the natural fibers: their characteristics, fabrics and uses, and care instructions.

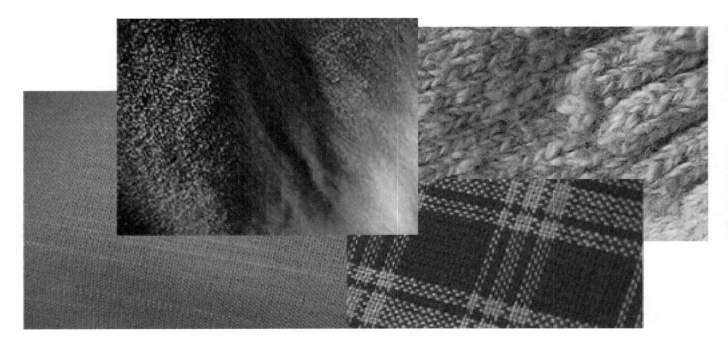

FIBER AND SOURCE	CHARACTERISTICS	TYPICAL FABRICS AND USES	CARE INSTRUCTIONS
Cotton	Strong, even when wet. Comfortable, absorbent. Draws heat from body. Dyes easily. Shrinks unless treated. Will deteriorate from mildew. Tendency to wrinkle. Weakened by sunlight.	Versatile in weight, texture, and construction Used for summer wear, work clothes, and in heavier weights for warm, seasonal clothes. Examples: Corduroy, poplin terry, seersucker, broadcloth, denim, organdy, tweed.	Most colorfast cottons can be washed in hot water, others in warm or cold water. Bleach may be used on whites. Fabric softener will reduce wrinkling. Tumble dry at hot setting. Iron while damp or use steam iron.
Linen	Very strong, but stiff; may show wear at the edges and folds. Absorbent. Draws heat from body. Wrinkles easily. Hard to dye. Tendency to shrink and stretch. Will deteriorate from mildew but not moths.	Fabrics usually have a course texture and natural luster. Weave weights vary from very light to heavy. Used for summer dresses, blouses, and suiting. It is also used in many household items.	Usually dry-cleaned to keep its freshness. Can be washed if preshrunk.
Silk	Strong, absorbent, and holds in body heat. Wrinkle resistant. Dyes easily, but may bleed. Resists mildew and moths. Weakened by sunlight and perspiration.	Luxurious, lustrous fabrics in many weights from sheer, drapable chiffon to stiff, rich brocades in brilliant colors and beautiful prints. Used for dresses, suits, blouses, linings, lingerie. Examples: crepes, brocade, satin, jersey, tweed, chiffon.	Usually dry cleaned. If washable, usually done by hand in mild suds. Avoid chlorine bleach. Iron at low temperature setting.
Wool	Relatively weak and stretches when wet. Exceptionally absorbent. Holds in body heat. Wrinkles fall out. Dyes easily. Needs moth-proofing. Shrinks unless treated.	Versatile in weight, texture, weave, color. Tailors well due to the ability to be molded into shape. Used for sweaters, dresses, suits, and coats. Example: crepe, flannel, fleece, gabardine, tweed, jersey.	Usually dry cleaned. Many sweaters can be washed in tepid water and mild suds; do not use chlorine bleach. Some wools can be machine washed; follow manufacturer's instructions.

Answer the following questions.

3.1   What are the four main steps in fabric production? Explain what happens in each step.

   a. _____

   b. _____

   c. _____

   d. _____

3.2   _____ and _____ are the two types of fibers.

3.3   List the source for each of the following natural fibers.

   a. cotton _____

   b. linen _____

   c. silk _____

   d. wool _____

3.4   Which natural fiber is the weakest?_____

3.5   Which natural fiber does not dye easily? _____

3.6   Which two natural fibers draw heat from the body? _____ and _____

3.7   _____ and _____ are natural fibers which are less apt to wrinkle.

3.8   _____ needs moth proofing.

3.9   _____ is a fabric most likely to be used in household items.

3.10 _____ is used in the production of denim.

3.11 _____ is used in the production of lingerie.

3.12 _____ is used in the making of sweaters.

3.13 _____ requires no dry cleaning.

MAN-MADE FIBERS

For thousands of years, natural fibers were the only materials used to make fabric. In the middle of the nineteenth century, scientists started experimenting with the production of "artificial" silk from a natural source, cellulose. However, man-made fibers are actually a product of the twentieth century. "The chemical complexities of man-made fibers are endless, but one of the distinctions among them is the fact that some fibers are derived from natural materials such as **cellulose** or **protein**, while others are completely synthesized or developed from basic chemical sources."[6] Fibers made from natural sources include rayon and acetates. Some **synthetic** fibers are nylon, acrylics, polyester, and spandex.

Much confusion about synthetics comes from the numerous terms used to identify them. There is a generic name for the fiber type itself, and a company's trademark name for that fiber. For example, Orlon® and Acrilan® are both registered trademarks (of different companies) for an acrylic. Although trademark fibers may differ from others in its group, the basic characteristics will be the same.

The following chart lists the man-made fibers used in fabrics; note their characteristics, fabrics and uses, and care instructions.

6. *The Vogue Sewing Book*, Butterick Publishing, New York 1980. p 32

FIBER AND TRADEMARK	CHARACTERISTICS	TYPICAL FABRIC USES	CARE
Acetate Ariloft® Celanese® Chromspun® Estron® Loftura®	Relatively weak. Moderately absorbent. Holds in body heat. Tends to wrinkle. Dyes well. Resists pilling, shrinking, mildew, and moths. Weakened by light. Accumulates static.	Silk-like appearance, luxurious soft feel, excellent draping qualities. Used for lingerie, dresses, blouses, linings. Examples: satin, jersey, taffeta, lace, brocade, tricot, and crepe.	Usually dry cleaned. If washable use mild suds in warm or cold water at gentle speed. Tumble dry at lowest setting or hang up to dry. Hand wash, gently squeeze suds through fabric, and rinse in lukewarm water. Iron while damp with light pressure on wrong side at lowest temperature; a hot iron may melt the fabric. Do not use acetone (as in nail polish) or other organic solvents.
Acrylic Acrilan® Creslon® Fina® Orlon® Sefram®	Good wrinkle resistance. Holds in body heat. Lightweight, strong. May accumulate static electricity. Low absorbency, quick drying. Dyes well, color fast. Resists mildew, moths, chemicals, and sunlight. Holds shape well, good pleat retention.	Commonly soft, light, fluffy fabric construction. Used for dresses, sweaters, suits, sports and work clothes. Examples: sheer fabrics, knits, fleece, fur-like and pile fabrics.	Some acrylics can be dry-cleaned, but laundering is recommended. Can be machine-washed (warm setting), tumble-dried. Use water-softener to reduce static cling. Ironing is not necessary if removed from dryer promptly.
Glass Fiberglass	Strong. Non-absorbent. Resists wrinkles. Not easily dyed. Low abrasion resistance. Undamaged by many chemicals, sunlight.	Fabric types from sheer and lightweight to coarse and heavy. Used for curtains, draperies, and upholstery.	Hand laundering usually recommended. Chlorine bleach can be used for white fabrics. Ironing is not necessary as a rule.

Metallic Lurex® Metlon®	Weak. Non-absorbent. Tarnishes unless coated properly. Not affected by salt water, chlorinated water, or climatic conditions. Heat-sensitive.	First made into yarns; these are usually coated with plastic, polyester, or acetate film and made into gold, silver, and other colors of glittery fabric.	Launder or dry-clean according to care instructions. Do not use high temperature for either washing or ironing.
Modacrylic Acrilan® Elura® SEF® Verel®	Good wrinkle resistance. Exceptional strength. Holds in body heat. Resists moth, mildew. Non-allergenic. Very heat-sensitive, softens at low temperatures. Dries quickly. Flame-resistant.	Available in deep-pile fleece. and fur-like fabrics. Used for coats, linings, plush toys, carpets, and wigs. Example: Fake fur	Deep-pile should be dry-cleaned. For fabrics labeled "washable," follow care instructions. Avoid ironing.
Nylon Antron® Blue C® Caprolan® Celanese® Crepeset® Enkalure® Qiana® Zefran®	Strong, low absorbency. Holds in body heat. Resists shrinking, moths, and mildew. Tend to **pill.** Dyes easily, may fade in sun. Can be heat-set to hold shape, pleats, and embossed effects. Very elastic. Melts under high heat. Resistant to non-oily stains.	Wide range of fabric textures and weight from smooth and crisp to soft and bulky. Often blended with other fibers. Used for lingerie, linings, swimsuits, blouses, rainwear, and dresses. Examples: fake-fur, satin, jersey, and cire.	Can be washed by hand or machine in warm water, use gentle machine cycle. Use fabric softener to reduce static electricity. Tumble or drip-dry. Iron at low temperature.
Olefin Herculon® Marvess®	Holds in body heat. Soil resistant. Strong. Heat sensitive, melts easily. Non absorbent. Excellent elasticity and resiliency. Difficult to dye.	Fabrics are usually bulky, but lightweight, wool-like. Used for outerwear, filling, and upholstery.	Machine-wash, lukewarm water, use fabric softener in final rinse. Tumble-dry lowest setting. Iron at lowest temperature; use moderate setting for touch-ups.
Polyester Avlin® Blue C® Caprolan® Dacron® Fortel® Kodel® Quintess® Trevira® Vycron® Zefran®	Strong, low absorbency. Holds in body heat. Resists wrinkling, stretching, moths and mildew. Retains heat-set pleats. Accumulates static electricity. Wash & wear quick drying.	Wide variety of fabrics in many weights and constructions. Used for durable press (permanent press) and knit fabrics, found in suits, shirts, slacks, dresses, blouses, lingerie, thread, and filling for pillows.	Most polyesters are washable in warm water by hand or machine. Tumble or drip dry. Use fabric softener to reduce static electricity. May need little or no ironing; use moderate setting for touch ups.

Rayon Avril® Beau-Grip® Coloray® Enkrome® Fibro® Zantrel®	Relatively weak. Soft and comfortable. Absorbent. Holds in body heat. Easily dyed and generally colorfast. Wrinkles, shrinks or stretches unless treated.	Many fabrics weights, textures silky to coarse. Used for dresses, blouses, suits, linings, draperies. Example: Buthcer linen, matte jersey.	Many rayons need to be dry-cleaned. Some are washable in warm water, gentle machine cycle. Iron while damp and at moderate setting.
Spandex Lycra®	Strong and durable. Non-absorbent. Great elasticity. Lightweight. Easily dyed, may yellow with exposure to light.	Flexible lightweight fabrics. Used for foundation garments, swimwear, ski pants, and other sportswear; elastic banding.	Wash by hand or by machine using gentle cycle. Avoid chlorine bleach. Tumble or drip-dry at cool setting. Iron at low temperature.
Triacetate Arnel®	Relatively weak. Resists wrinkling and shrinking. Easily dyed. Retains heat set pleats.	Lightweight fabrics. Used for sportswear and skirts where pleat retention is desirable. Examples: Often found in blends such as tricot, shark-skin, flannel, and taffeta.	Hand or machine wash in warm water. Drip-dry pleated garments; tumble-dry other styles. Ironing usually required.

Answer the following questions.

3.14 When did scientists begin experimenting with "artificial" silk? _____

3.15 In what century did man-made fibers really start being produced? _____

3.16 Distinguish between man-made natural and synthesized fibers. _____

_____

3.17 Give an example of a man-made fiber that is made from natural sources. _____

3.18 Give an example of a synthesized fiber. _____

3.19 What is the generic name for the trademark name of Orlon®? _____

3.20 What is the trademark name of the generic name of Spandex? _____

3.21 Almost all synthetics, with the exception of rayon, are low in porosity and absorbency. What might we deduct from this statement? _____

Answer *true* **or** *false*.

3.22 _____ Synthetics are highly resilient and wrinkle resistant.

Review the material in this section in preparation for the Self Test. This Self Test will check your mastery of this particular section as well as your knowledge of the previous sections.

SELF TEST 3

List and explain each of the four steps in the production of fabric (each answer, 5 points).

3.01 _____

_____

_____

3.02 _____

_____

_____

3.03 _____

_____

_____

3.04 _____

_____

_____

List the source for the four natural fibers (each answer, 5 points).

3.05 cotton _____

3.06 linen _____

3.07 silk _____

3.08 wool _____

Matching (each answer, 3 points) **NOTE:** there may be more than one answer.

3.09 _____ draws heat from the body   a. cotton

3.010 _____ needs moth proofing   b. linen

3.011 _____ does not dye easily   c. silk

3.012 _____ used in making sweaters   d. wool

3.013 _____ its fabric is used for lingerie

3.014 _____ less apt to wrinkle

3.015 _____ requires no dry cleaning

Answer *true* or *false* (each answer, 2 points).

3.016 _____ Man-made fibers really started being produced in the twentieth century.

3.017 _____ Synthesized fibers are made from natural sources.

3.018 _____ Rayon is an example of a synthesized fiber.

3.019 _____ Polyester is an example of a synthesized fiber.

3.020 _____ Cellulose is found in the cell wall of wood, cottons, and hemp.

3.021 _____ Orlon is a trademark name.

3.022 _____ Acrylic is a trademark name.

3.023 _____ Rayons are low in porosity and absorbency so they are not comfortable to wear in hot or humid weather.

3.024 _____ Synthetics are wrinkle-resistant.

3.025 _____ Status is gained when clothing is able to give a person a higher rank in society.

3.026 _____ Adornment refers to dress codes and individuality.

3.027 _____ A fad is the direction in which fashion is moving.

3.028 _____ Some experts attribute the rise and fall of the hemline to the stock market.

3.029 _____ Yellow is a secondary color.

3.030 _____ Hue is the term referring to the name of a color.

3.031 _____ A mandarin collar is a rolled collar.

3.032 _____ A short person should wear horizontal lines.

3.033 _____ Cool colors make a person appear thinner.

3.034 _____ A parka is a heavy winter jacket with a hood.

3.035 _____ Composite garments are made by combining tailored and draped methods of construction.

81 / 101

Score _____

Adult Check _____

Initial   Date

IV. CARE OF CLOTHES

Everything in the closet should be ready to wear. When an item is dirty, wash or clean it; when it's ripped, mend it. When an article of clothing becomes outdated, worn out, too small or large, give it away. Learning to adequately care for your clothes is vital for maintaining a useful and sharp-appearing wardrobe.

SECTION OBJECTIVES

Review these objectives. When you have completed this section, you should be able to:

   9. Demonstrate various mending techniques.

   10. Demonstrate the ability to launder clothing.

MENDING

This section gives emphasis to the many diversified methods of repairing or mending clothes. With all the modern techniques and products available today, mending clothes is not as time-consuming or as difficult as it used to be. Sewing machines have increased capabilities. There are **fusible** mending aids, fabric glue, and portable mending appliances as well. Using these products and techniques does not mean sacrificing quality; these products result in sturdy repair, often less visible than one done by a more traditional method.

Mending includes all sorts of repairs to damaged garments. Threads weaken, seams split, buttons loosen or fall off, knees and elbows on pants and shirts may wear thin, zippers break, hems become undone, and knits snag. All of these problems are fixable with very little effort.

Make mending fun by using your creative side. For example, use pockets, a row of trim, appliqué, decorative button, or a non-functional zipper instead of a patch to hide a hole, tear, or to reinforce a worn spot.

As with any craft, there are tools that are needed to accomplish the task. Following is a list of the tools and supplies needed for a basic mending kit. You can organize your supplies in a small sewing basket, decorative tin, or fishing tackle box. This will be a great item to have when you go to college. Although the sewing machine is used for many mending jobs and will be referred to in this section, we will discuss the sewing machine and its parts in more detail in LIFEPAC 5.

fig. a

fig. b

fig. c

fig. d

fig. e

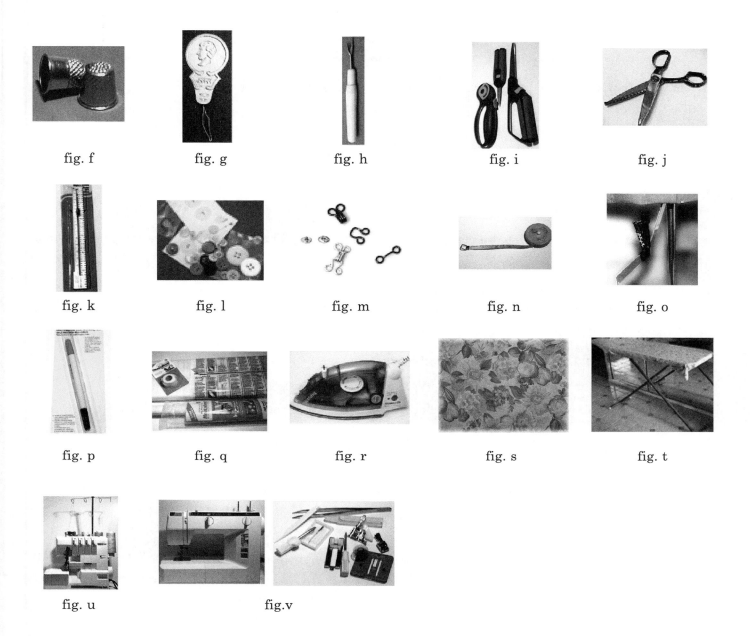

fig. f	fig. g	fig. h	fig. i	fig. j
fig. k	fig. l	fig. m	fig. n	fig. o
fig. p	fig. q	fig. r	fig. s	fig. t
fig. u	fig.v			

Hand needles (fig. a). For general sewing, use sharps, medium-length needles with small round eyes and sharp points. Keep a package of assorted sizes (3-9) on hand.

Pins (fig. b). Size 17 steel dressmaker pins will not rust and are an all-purpose size. Throw away pins that are bent or have become dull because they can damage or snag fabric.

Safety Pins (fig. c). Safety pins should not be used for permanent repair, but an assortment of sizes are important for emergency mending.

Thread (fig. d). Five basic colors of thread will cover most mending needs. Choose a dark color in your basic wardrobe color (black, navy blue, or brown). Add spools of white, red, medium gray, and a transparent **monofilament** thread which can be used with any color of fabric.

Beeswax or white candle stub (fig. e). Before hand sewing, pull thread across one of these waxy substances to reduce knotting and tangling.

Thimble (fig f). Wear a thimble on your middle finger while hand sewing. Make sure it fits snugly.

Needle threader (fig. g). This flexible wire loop slips through the eye of the needle for easy threading. It can also be used for pulling knit snags to the wrong side.

Seam ripper (fig. h). This tool makes it easy to cut seams open, rip hems, and remove stitching. Use the pointed end for removing cut threads.

Scissors (fig. i). Good quality 6" scissors with one sharp point are essential for clipping, snipping, and trimming. Use these scissors only for sewing to keep the blades sharp.

Pinking shears (fig. j). Excellent instrument for finishing seams and raw edges. They cut zigzag, producing a ravel-resistant edge.

Seam gauge (fig. k). Use a 6" seam gauge with a sliding marker for making small measurements such as hems and button locations.

Extra buttons (fig. l). Keep a small container of buttons in basic styles and colors to replace lost and broken buttons. It is a good idea to store any extra buttons that come with garments, along with the laundering instructions, in a file.

Hooks, eyes, snaps (fig. m). Have on hand assorted sizes in nickel and black finish for light and dark fabrics.

Tape measure (fig. n). Use a 60" flexible cloth or plastic tape for body and garment measurements.

Yardstick or skirt marker (fig. o). A skirt marker is a ruler that stands upright on a base. A sliding marker can be positioned the desired distance from the floor to ensure even hems.

Liquid marking pencil (fig. p). Felt-tip pens for making the placement of trims, hems, and alterations are available in two types. One type leaves a mark that fades and disappears within a few hours; the other rinses out easily with water.

Fusible web, iron-on patches, and appliqués (fig. q). Fusible web is a non-woven bonding agent available in strips and sheets. Place it between two layers of fabric, then press with an iron to melt the web and bond the layers. Iron-on patches are available in basic colors. Use precut iron-on shapes or purchase large pieces to be cut to desired size. Iron-on appliqués are an instant way to cover holes and tears in children's clothing.

Steam/dry iron (fig. r). Fusible and iron-on mending materials make the iron a valuable mending aid. Be sure to use a press cloth to protect the surface of your iron. Your iron will play an important role in pressing seams open, darts down, etc. when you begin sewing your own clothes.

Press cloth (fig. s). Use a lint-free press cloth when adhering fusible interfacing and when pressing on the right side of a garment.

Regular or tabletop ironing board (fig. t). Use the table top ironing board on a table or countertop for small pressing jobs. It is also a great item to have for college. Use a regular ironing board for larger tasks.

Button sewer or serger (fig. u). (optional) This appliance speeds sewing on flat buttons. It can also be used for tacking seams and hems.

Sewing machine and accessories (fig. v). (optional) Repair clothing with the machine whenever possible to save time and achieve sturdier, better-looking results.

Answer the following questions.

4.1 _____ are medium-length needles with round eyes and sharp points.

4.2 Why should you throw away pins that have become dull?_____

4.3 What purpose do safety pins serve? _____ For what are they NOT used?

_____

4.4 What five colors of thread should you have in a basic mending kit?_____

_____

4.5 What is transparent monofilament thread? _____

4.6 The pointed end of a seam ripper is for _____ .

4.7 Describe a good pair of sewing scissors. _____

4.8 A good tape measure should be _____ long.

Although there are numerous mending tasks that will present themselves to you over the years, we will look at some of the basic ones here to get you started. The most frequent problem is likely to be a loose or lost button. A button that is sewn on securely and correctly should last the life of the garment. To prevent the loss of a loose button, resew it as soon as you notice threads are starting to **fray**. Usually if one button is loose, the others on the garment are soon to follow, so check all buttons when you resew one.

There are two types of buttons, flat or sew-through buttons and shank buttons. Shank buttons are those that have a little "neck" or shank with a hole in it on the lower side. This shank allows the button to sit on top of the buttonhole instead of crowding to the inside and distorting the buttonhole. The shank is recommended for closures in heavy and bulky fabrics.

For all hand-sewn buttons, cut the thread about 30" long, run it over beeswax, fold the thread in half and insert folded edge into eye of needle. Knot the cut ends together. Mark the position of the button with a few stitches. Place the button on the markings and stitch according to the directions for each type of button.

shank buttons

flat buttons

A sewing machine may be used to attach buttons on light to medium-weight fabrics. Check the instruction manual for instructions. A button sewer attaches buttons quickly and easily as well.

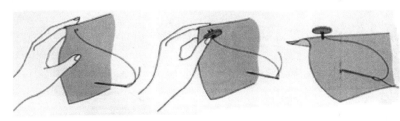

Flat button. To sew a flat button to a garment, center the button over the marking and sew in place through the holes in button. Fasten stitches on wrong side of garment. Flat buttons with four holes may be sewn with stitches that cross in the center, form a square or parallel lines, or radiate from one hole.

Shank button. To sew a shank button to a garment, make several stitches through the shank and fabric. Secure the thread with two small stitches under the shank.

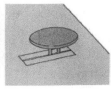   

Flat button with thread shank. To sew a flat button with a thread shank to a garment, secure the thread at the button marking, then bring needle up through one hole in button. Lay a pin or toothpick across the top of the button. Take the needle

down through second hole, making about six stitches. Remove the pin or toothpick, lift button away from fabric so stitches are taut, and wind thread firmly around the stitches to make the shank. Backstitch into shank to secure thread.

Answer the following questions.

4.9 Two types of buttons are _____ and _____ .

4.10 What is the purpose of the shank on a button?_____

4.11 The shank is recommended for closures in _____ and _____ fabrics.

Complete the following activity.

Student: You will begin to make your *Sewing Skills Notebook*. You will be adding many pages to this notebook from the unit on mending and then skills demonstrated from the lessons in LIFEPAC 5. I suggest a loose-leaf notebook with plain white paper to attach each piece of fabric. Fabric should be cut with pinking shears to prevent unraveling. Place glue on one edge of the fabric about 1/2" to 1" wide and stick on the sheet in your *Sewing Skills Notebook*. It is important to leave the material loose on three sides so the teacher can check both the wrong as well as the right sides of your sewing. Label each page with the skill(s) that is being demonstrated.

4.12 Using a six-inch square piece of fabric, fold over one edge about 1" to 1 1/2" for extra strength. Demonstrate your skills in sewing on a flat button, a shank button, and a flat button with a thread shank. Place on the first page of your *Sewing Skills Notebook*.

 Adult Check _____

Initial   Date

Fasteners such as snaps and hooks and eyes may have to be resewn if they become loose or they may have to be replaced. Sometimes a more sturdy fastener is needed to replace one that is not strong enough for the amount of stress put on it. If the garment is too tight, it may be possible to just move the fastener over slightly.

Snaps should be used only when there is little stress put on the closure. A snap that does not stay closed may be replaced with a larger, heavy-duty snap or with a hook and eye. Heavy-duty snaps can replace ordinary snaps or overlapping hooks and eyes on sturdy, heavyweight fabrics. They are applied with special snap pliers or a hammer and small tool as specified on the package.

Hooks and eyes are usually used on waistbands or above a zipper where they are inconspicuous. If the finished edges just meet, use a hook with a round eye; if the edges overlap, use a hook with a straight eye.

Use two sets for strength on a waistband. Heavy-duty hooks and eyes (also called skirt hooks and eyes) are used on waistbands as a sturdier closure than ordinary hook and eyes. These hooks are strong and flat so they will not slide out of the eye.

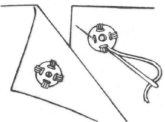

Snaps. Attach ball section to the underside overlap far enough in from the edge so it will not show. Position the socket section on the right side of the underlap to align with the ball. Using a single strand of waxed thread, secure thread at snap location. Take three or four straight stitches up through each hole; do not stitch through to right side of garment. Secure thread with tiny stitches in fabric at last hole.

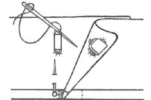

Regular hook and eye. Sew hook on underside of overlap without stitching through to right side. Using single strand of waxed thread, take four or five stitches through each hole. Take two or three stitches across the end, under the hook, to hold it flat. Position eye in place and tack through holes as for the hook. Secure thread on underside.

Heavy-duty hook and eye. Position and sew on the hook and eye as for a regular lapped hook and eye. You do not need to secure the end of the hook.

 Answer the following questions.

4.13   Which type of fastener is best for waistbands? _____

4.14   Which type of fastener is the weakest?_____

4.15   Which type of eye do you use if the edges overlap?_____

4.16   Besides strength, what is the advantage of using a heavy-duty hook and eye?_____
        _____

Complete the following activity.

4.17   Demonstrate your skills in sewing on a snap, hook and eye and a heavy-duty hook and eye. Follow these steps carefully.
    •   Cut three strips of fabric 10" by 3".
    •   Cut each strip in half lengthwise, making three sets of 5" by 3" pieces of fabric.
    •   Fold under 1½" on the short edge for strength on all six pieces.
    •   Overlapping the folded edges, sew a regular hook and eye on the inside edge of one piece of fabric and an eye on outside edge of the other piece of fabric.
    •   Repeat the process for the heavy-duty hook and eye and the snap.
    •   Glue the unfolded edges of the pieces of fabric into your *Sewing Skills Notebook* making sure that the fasteners are hooked or snapped, forming a secure closure.

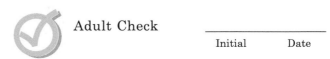

Adult Check   _____
                   Initial   Date

Repairing a split seam is another very common mending task. The simplest remedy is to repair it with a straight stitch on a sewing machine. If a sewing machine is not available, a simple backstitch by hand works nicely as well.

A backstitch is a strong hand-stitch that duplicates machine stitching. Take small stitches, working from right to left, inserting needle behind the previous stitch. Bring needle up same distance in front of stitch. Continue to insert and bring up needle half a stitch length behind and in front of previous stitch.

Seams in knit or actionwear garments often split because they are sewn with thread that was not strong enough to "give" with the natural elasticity of the fabric or a straight stitch was used when a special stretch stitch should have been applied.

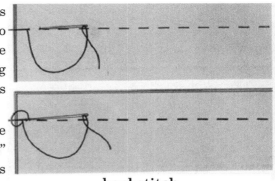

backstitch

Certain seams often wear out and split before others in a garment. These are the stress seams and include seams in the crotch, underarm, and pockets. When these seams split, they should be repaired with smaller stitches, two rows of stitching, or machine reinforcement stitching.

Answer the following questions.

4.18 What is the easiest method of repairing a ripped seam? _____

4.19 What kind of hand-stitch works best for repairing a ripped seam? _____

4.20 What kind of stitch works best to repair a ripped seam in a knit fabric? _____

4.21 What are examples of stress seams? _____

_____

4.22 How can you best repair a stress seam? _____

Complete the following activity.

4.23 Demonstrate your skill in hand-sewing a seam. Cut a six inch square piece of fabric. Fold in half and stitch the open seam together using a backstitch, ⁵/₈″ from open edge. Glue the <u>folded</u> edge of the piece of fabric into your *Sewing Skills Notebook*.

Adult Check _____

Initial   Date

It takes only minutes to repair a hem that has pulled out. Make emergency repairs with double-faced mending tape, fabric glue, or a portable hem-and-tacker.

Non-sewing repairs can be made with strips of fusible web. This permanent hem withstands washing and dry-cleaning.

Hand-stitching the repair gives a custom finish. Use blindstitch for woven, ragged fabrics finished with **seam binding** or an **overcast edge**; catchstitch is durable for flat hems in pants, knits, and heavy fabrics. Use slipstitch for woven fabrics with a **turned-under** edge.

Machine-stitched repair takes less time and is stronger than hand stitching, and it gives a professional looking finish. Machine blindstitch provides an invisible hem. A straight-stitched hem shows on the right side.

EMERGENCY REPAIRS

Double-faced mending tape. You do not need an iron for this method. Place tape on garment with edge along hemming line; leave backing on tape. Press firmly with fingers. Remove paper back. Fold hem up at ends of tape and pinch in place. Smooth hem, applying pressure from center outward. Remove tape before washing or dry-cleaning.

Fabric glue. Test for staining in a hidden area. Spread foil under fabric to protect the work surface. Apply a thin line of glue to hem edge. Spread lightly with finger or tube tip. Fold hem in place. Blot excess with damp cloth. Apply light pressure with fingers or use straight pins to hold. Glue dries in five minutes. It is washable but not dry-cleanable.

Fusible web. Apply web strips (1/2" to 3/4" wide) between two layers of fabric. Steam press with damp press cloth as directed on package.

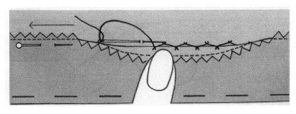
blindstitch

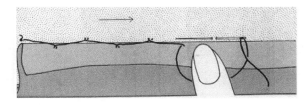
catchstitch

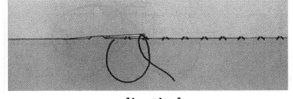
slipstitch

HAND STITCH REPAIRS

Blindstitch. This hand stitch can be used on a pinked, overcast edges or seam-taped hem. Work from right to left. Roll hem edge back about 1/4". Take a tiny stitch in the garment. Take next stitch in hem 1/4" to 1/2" to left of first stitch. Continue alternating stitches. Keep stitches in garment small and do not pull too tightly. When you are done, the roll hem edge will hide the stitches.

Catchstitch. This hand stitch is used on knits and heavy fabrics to provide give and to hold hem edge flat to garment. Work from left to right. Take a small horizontal stitch in hem edge. Take next stitch in garment about 1/4" to right, crossing the stitches.

Slipstitch. Use this hand stitch to join two edges when a nearly invisible stitch is desired. One edge must be on a fold. Working from right to left, slip needle through fold for about 1/4". Then take stitch directly opposite fold, catching only one or two threads of the garment fabric. Continue stitching, alternating between fold and fabric.

MACHINE REPAIR

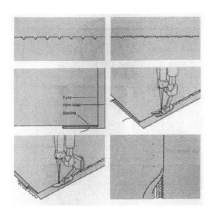

Machine blindstitch. This is for sturdy hems. Baste hem to garment 1/4" from raw edge. Adjust machine to blindstitch setting and attach blindstitch foot or zigzag foot with hemming guide. Place hem face down and fold garment back to basting line. Stitch close to the fold, catching garment only in wide zigzag stitch. Press flat. This takes practice so do not get discouraged. This is the best method for pants.

Straight stitch. This machine stitch is used to hem and finish raw edges in one step or to add decorative detail. Turn up hem 1 1/2" and pin in place. For ragged fabrics, pink or turn under raw edge. On right side, topstitch 1" from folded edge. As a design detail, add a second or third row of stitches.

Answer the following questions.

4.24   Double-faced mending tape and fabric glue are two ways to make _____ repairs on a hem.

4.25   Fusible web is a _____ repair method of hemming that can be both washed and

_____ .

4.26   Which hand stitch method for hem repairs works best for a fold? _____

4.27   Which hand stitch method for hem repairs works best for pants, knits, and heavy fabrics?

_____ .

4.28   Which method for hem repairs is the most hidden and works well with an overcast edge?

_____ .

4.29   Which machine stitch method of hemming shows on the outside of the garment? _____

Complete the following activity.

4.30   Demonstrate your skills for repairing hems by doing each of the following tasks.
        You will need a 6″ square of fabric for each task.
   •   Make a temporary hem by using double-faced mending tape.
   •   Make a permanent hem, using the non-sewing method fusible web.
   •   Sew a blindstitch hem by hand.
   •   Sew a catchstitch hem by hand.
   •   Sew a slipstitch hem by hand.
   •   Sew a blindstitch hem by machine.
   •   Sew a straight-stitch hem by machine.

Glue each piece of fabric with the finished hem on a separate sheet of paper in your *Sewing Skills Notebook*. Be sure to label each sheet.

Adult Check   _____
                    Initial   Date

LAUNDERING

All manufacturers are required by law (the federal Care Labeling Rule, revised in 1984) to attach permanent care labels on their garments and fabrics sold by the yard. It is located at the end of the fabric bolt or roll. Record these instructions and add them to your card file of hang tags and garment notions. Some fabric stores have small care information tags available at the fabric cutting counter. Ask for these when you purchase fabrics and sew them right onto the garments you make.

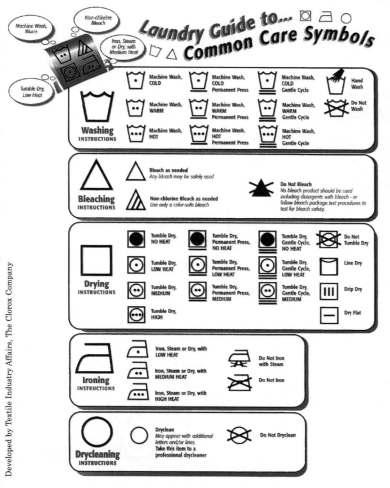

The fabric your clothing is made of comes from fibers, which are made into yarns, yarns into fabric, and fabric into clothing. Although the chart supplied in Section III describes the care for each fiber, care is also affected by fabric construction, finishes, and garment assembly. All these affect the content of the care labels. Therefore, garments made of identical fibers may have different care instructions.

Planning one's washing and drying ahead of time saves time and results in cleaner clothes. Preparation helps prevent shrinkage, bleeding, fading, stretching, linting, pilling, snags, and broken zippers.

Although some washable garments require hand washing (See "How To Wash

HAND WASH
SEPARATELY
COLD WATER
TUMBLE DRY LOW
NO BLEACH

MACHINE WASH
WARM
WITH LIKE COLORS
DELICATE CYCLE
ONLY NON-
CHLORINE BLEACH
WHEN NEEDED
TUMBLE DRY
LOW

MACHINE WASH COLD
GENTLE CYCLE
TUMBLE DRY
UNTIL DAMP
RESHAPE AND
DRY FLAT
USE ONLY
NON-CHLORINE
BLEACH WHEN NEEDED
WARM IRON AS NEEDED
VER AL DORSO PARA
CUIDADO

55% RAMIE
45% ACRYLIC
MADE IN HONG KONG
RN 54590
HAND OR MACHINE
WASH IN COLD WATER
GENTLE CYCLE
USE MILD SOAP
TUMBLE DRY LOW
DO NOT USE BLEACH
DO NOT DRY CLEAN

MADE IN U.S.A
RN 82936
100% POLYESTER
MACHINE WASH COLD
TUMBLE DRY LOW NO
BLEACH COOL IRON
COB #000682
MFR #907954
LARGE

Clothes By Hand") most can be machine washed. Most washing machines have settings for hot, warm, or cold water; permanent press, delicate, and normal cycles; and varying water levels for different load sizes. Home dryers have at least two temperature settings and several cycles that are either timed or automatically sensitive to dryness, including an air dry cycle that tumbles clothes without using heat.

First, look over the articles you plan to wash to be sure there is no jewelry, ribbon, or trimming that should be removed or anything in the pockets. Mend any rips, tears, snags, or loose buttons before washing to prevent further damage. Close zippers, hooks, and buttons to prevent snags. For cleaner collars and cuffs, turn shirts inside out and button the top button.

Then, sort the clothes. Sort them by color, fabric, bulk, and degree of soil. Wash white fabrics separately, for they can become dingy when washed with colors. Separate colorfast items from dark or bright colors that may bleed. Wash similar colors in the same load. Separate man-made fibers (nylon, spandex, etc.) from natural fibers. Separate delicates such as knits, laces, and sheers. Separate fabrics that create a good deal of lint (fleece, terrycloth) from those that don't. Sort by bulk, for they need enough space in the washer to move freely. One king- or queen-size sheet, twin sheet, and a few small items fills an average washer. Separate the slightly soiled from the very dirty.

Read the care instruction labels of all garments before you launder them. Some need special treatment: no chlorine bleach, extra soaking, no tumble drying, etc. Use the correct temperature water for the garment's fabric and fiber. Most cottons and preshrunk linens can be washed in hot water. Man-made fibers usually require cold or warm water. Pre-treat stains and heavily soiled areas before washing (See stain removal chart on the next page). Note if the garment needs an extra rinse cycle and/or special drying instructions.

HOW TO WASH CLOTHES BY HAND

Remove your rings and be sure that your hands are clean. Prepare the garment the same as you would for machine-washing; look for jewelry and anything else that should be removed, sort clothes, pre-treat stains and decide on the water temperature you should use for each garment.

In a sink or bowl that is partly filled with water, dissolve enough liquid soap or powdered detergent to make good suds. Squeeze the sudsy water through the garment gently without rubbing or twisting it. Badly soiled clothes may require more than one sudsing and a little rubbing on the soiled spots.

Rinse the garment two or three times in clear water of the same temperature to remove all traces of soap or detergent.

Gently squeeze excess water out of the garment. **NOTE:** If the garment is made of drip-dry fabric, take special care not to wring or twist it. While it is still wet, place it on a rustproof hanger and allow it to drip dry. Since drip-dry garments require little or no ironing, smooth the seams, cuffs and collar with the hands while it is still wet. Some garments will need to lay flat rather than drip dry to prevent stretching or losing their shape.

When you want a garment to dry quickly, spread out a bath towel, place the garment on it, roll up the garment and the towel together, and gently press out the excess water. Unroll at once.

STAIN REMOVAL CHART

STAIN	WHAT YOU NEED	WHAT YOU DO
Blood	Cold water, warm suds	Soak in cold water, wash in warm (not hot) suds, and rinse well.
Chewing gum	a. Ice, knife b. Cleaning fluid	a. Rub spot with piece of ice until gum hardens. Scrape off with knife. b. Sponge with fluid if stain remains.
Chocolate or cocoa	Hot water, hot suds	Dip stained area in hot water and wash in hot suds.
Fruit juices, coffee, or tea	Cold water, boiling water, bowl	Soak in cold water. Stretch stained portion over empty bowl. Pour on boiling water from height of 1 to 2 feet.
Grease from foods, cold cream	a. Cleaning fluid, warm suds b. French chalk, cornstarch, or talc (on light fabrics only) c. Clean white blotting paper, warm iron	a. Sponge with cleaning fluid and wash in warm suds. b. Sprinkle grease spot with a chalk white powdery cleaner and let stand several hours. Brush off. Repeat if needed. c. Place stains between blotters and press blotter with warm iron.
Grease from machinery	Petroleum jelly or fat, warm suds	Rub petroleum jelly or fat into stain to soften. Wash in warm suds.
Ink (non-washable)	Milk, bowl	Soak stain in bowl of milk until milk sours. Repeat if needed. Wash in warm suds.
Ink (washable)	Cold water	Soak in water, rubbing and changing water as necessary. Another method is to spray aerosol hair spray on stain before washing.
Lipstick (if fabric is washable)	Petroleum jelly, warm suds	Rub petroleum jelly into stain. Wash in warm suds.
Mud	Warm suds, brush	When mud is dry, brush off as much as possible. Wash stain in warm suds and rinse.

Nail polish	Nail-polish remover (except for acetate fabric)	Sponge with polish remover.
Paint (if fresh)	Turpentine, warm suds	Rub spot lightly with cloth dipped in turpentine. Wash in warm suds.
Syrup or candy	Hot water	Soak in hot water and wash.

Answer the following questions.

4.31 What federal law requires manufacturers to put care labels on their garments and fabrics sold by the yard?_____

4.32 What is the unique feature of the air tumble cycle on a clothes dryer?_____

4.33 What is the first step for washing clothes? _____

4.34 What is the best way to have cleaner collars and cuffs on shirts? _____

_____

4.35 Clothes should be sorted by _____ , fabric, bulk and _____

_____

Answer *true* **or** *false*.

4.36 _____ Garments made of identical fibers may have different care instructions.

4.37 _____ Wring out excess water from hand washed garments so they will dry faster.

Complete the following activity.

4.38 Sort the clothes listed below into the proper wash loads. Use the fiber charts in section 3 as well as the rules for sorting clothing. Clothes that are made from man-made fibers and do not have specific generic or trademark names may be considered polyester blends.

Two cotton bath towels	Maroon slacks	Fiberglass curtains
Beige knit shirt	Navy blue shorts	Polyester shell with silver
Black suit jacket (lightweight)	Nylon pastel blouse	glitter sequins
Blanket	Nylon pastel undergarments	Fitted full bed sheet
Cotton corduroy pants	Pastel dress shirt	Purple shirt
Dark blue slacks	Pastel floral dress	Flat full bed sheet
Denim shirt	Two large pillowcases	Rayon dress
Denim skirt	Pink Dacron® dress	Fleece coat
Cotton dish cloths	Cotton dish towels	Red dress
Light green swimsuit	Arnel® cheerleader skirt (pleats)	Lavender negligee

Two cotton wash cloths   Tan dress slacks   Taffeta formal
Light blue knit jersey pullover   Linen suit (preshrunk)   Lavender dress
Yellow Qiana® blouse   Knit yellow/white basketball   Wool blend sweater
Two cotton hand towels   jersey   Light blue spandex shorts

Cotton—hot water

a. _____

b. _____

c. _____

d. _____

e. _____

Cotton/Linen—warm/cool water

a. _____

b. _____

c. _____

d. _____

Delicate/knits

a. _____

b. _____

c. _____

d. _____

e. _____

f. _____

g. _____

h. _____

Hand wash or gentle machine

a. _____

b. _____

c. _____

Permanent press—light colors

a. _____

b. _____

c. _____

d. _____

e. _____

f. _____

Permanent press—dark colors

a. _____

b. _____

c. _____

d. _____

e. _____

f. _____

Large Permanent Press

a. _____

b. _____

c. _____

(too large, needs its own load)

a. _____

Dry Clean

a. _____

b. _____

c. _____

d. _____

The last phase of laundering your clothes is ironing and pressing. Ironing and pressing not only reduces wrinkles in clothing, but also helps to retain details of tailoring such as creased pants legs, a smooth placket, and crisp pleats.

Ironing is the act of gliding the iron over the cloth, while pressing is raising and lowering the iron onto the fabric without any gliding motion. Always iron with straight strokes, either lengthwise or crosswise to the fabric grain. Circular or diagonal motion may stretch the fabric. Do not let the iron rest on the fabric.

Use the narrow end of the ironing board for things that must be slipped over it for ironing, and use the wide end for all flat ironing. Smooth out the items on the ironing board before ironing.

Test the temperature of the iron on some inner part of the garment with a pressing cloth placed over the garment. Iron fabrics until they are completely dry. Iron fabrics on the wrong side if they tend to become shiny.

Double over sheets or iron four thicknesses at once. Fold them lengthwise, then crosswise, with top hem on the outside. Iron pillowcases from closed end toward hem.

Place embroidered designs face down on a thick terry towel and iron on the wrong side.

Iron collars, sleeves, yokes, pockets, and trimming before ironing the body of the garment such as a dress or shirt. A sleeve board is useful in ironing sleeves and some collars.

When ironing or pressing garments, avoid wrinkling parts that have already been ironed. After ironing the garment, touch up important parts, such as the collar and cuffs. Be sure ironed clothing is dry and cool before storing. Place the finished garment on a hanger, closing the fasteners so as to retain the shape.

Answer the following questions.

4.39 _____ is gliding the iron over the material and _____ is raising and lowering the iron onto the fabric without any gliding motion.

4.40 Why should you NOT iron with a circular or diagonal motion?_____

4.41 What is the use of the narrow end of the ironing board? _____

4.42 How can you test if you have the iron at the right temperature for the garment you are going to iron?_____

4.43 How should you iron pillowcases? _____

4.44 On a shirt or dress, which is ironed first? _____

Before you take this last Self Test, you may want to do one or more of these self checks.

1. _____ Read the objectives. Determine if you can do them.

2. _____ Restudy the material related to any objectives that you cannot do.

3. _____ Use the SQ3R study procedure to review the material:
   a. **S**can the sections.
   b. **Q**uestion yourself again.
   c. **R**ead to answer your questions.
   d. **R**ecite the answers to yourself.
   e. **R**eview areas you didn't understand.

4. _____ Review all vocabulary, activities and Self Tests, writing a correct answer for each wrong answer.

SELF TEST 4

Matching (each answer, 3 points).

4.01 _____ used for small measurements, stitches, hems, and buttons   a. safety pins

4.02 _____ transparent monofilament   b. scissors

4.03 _____ essential for clipping, snipping, and trimming   c. fusible web

4.04 _____ used for finishing seams and raw edges   d. seam gauge

4.05 _____ reduces knotting and tangling of thread   e. pinking shears

4.06 _____ should not be used for permanent repair   f. thimble

4.07 _____ wear on middle finger while hand-sewing   g. thread

4.08 _____ saves time and achieves sturdier, better looking repair results   h. sewing machine

4.09 _____ non-woven bonding agent   i. seam ripper

4.010 _____ used to cut seams open, rip hems, and remove stitching   j. beeswax

Choose the correct letter (each answer, 3 points).

4.011 _____ are medium length needles with round eyes and sharp points.
- a. Steels   b. Sharps
- c. Points   d. Snaps

4.012 Safety pins _____ .
- a. should not be used for permanent repairs
- b. should be used for emergency repairs
- c. should be part of a basic repair kit in a variety of sizes
- d. none of the above
- e. all of the above

4.013 The pointed end of the seam ripper is used for _____ .
- a. cutting seams open   b. removing cut threads
- c. ripping hems   d. replacing buttons

4.014 The shank button _____ .
- a. is used for closures in light fabrics   b. lays flat against the fabric
- c. sits on top of the buttonhole   d. has four holes

4.015 Which of the following is NOT an example of a stress seam? _____
- a. underarm seam   b. pocket seams
- c. side seam   d. crotch seam

4.016 A _____ is the best hand stitch to use in mending a ripped seam.
- a. backstitch   b. blindstitch
- c. catchstitch   d. slipstitch

4.017 A _____ is the best hand stitch to use in mending a hem.
  a. backstitch   b. blindstitch
  c. catchstitch   d. slipstitch

4.018 The _____ is the hemming hand stitch which works best with an overcast edge.
  a. backstitch   b. blindstitch
  c. catchstitch   d. slipstitch

4.019 A _____ is the best hand stitch for hemming heavy fabrics and knits.
  a. backstitch   b. blindstitch
  c. catchstitch   d. slipstitch

4.020 Which statement is NOT true concerning laundering clothes? _____
  a. Garments made of identical fibers may have different care instructions.
  b. The federal Care Labeling Rule requires manufacturers to put care labels on garments
      and fabrics by the yard.
  c. Close zippers on garments before washing.
  d. Wring out excess water on hand-washed garments.

Complete the following (answer, 4 points).

4.021 Sort clothes by:

  a. _____

  b. _____

  c. _____

  d. _____

Fill in the blank (each answer, 4 points).

4.022 A tape measure should be _____ long.

4.023 _____ are the type of fasteners that work best for low stress closures.

4.024 Ironing in a circular or diagonal motion can cause the fabric to _____ .

4.025 _____ is good for removal of non-washable ink stains.

4.026 _____ is a natural fiber that can be washed in hot water.

4.027 Knits, laces and sheers require a _____ washing cycle.

Score _____

Adult Check _____
Initial   Date

GLOSSARY

accentuate. To give emphasis or prominence.

accessories. Articles of dress such as gloves, earrings or scarf that add completeness, convenience, attractiveness, etc. to one's basic apparel.

attire. Clothes or apparel.

attitudes. Person's feelings about or reactions to people, things and ideas as formed from the person's values.

beauty. A quality that gives pleasure to the senses and creates a positive emotional reaction in the viewer.

cellulose. Inert carbohydrate found in the cell walls of wood, cotton, hemp, etc.

conformity. Act of obeying or agreeing with some given standard or authority.

countenance. Appearance, especially the facial expression.

dress codes. Written or unwritten rules of what should or should not be worn by a group of people.

elements. Weather, climate, seasonal changes.

first impressions. What you think of a person, thing or idea based on appearance, walk and talk.

fray. Raveled threads or fibers at the edge or end.

fusible. Capable of being fused or melted by heating.

gradation. Gradual increase or decrease in size, color, texture or number.

guises. Assumed appearance or mere semblance (likeness, image or copy).

opposition. When lines meet to form right angles. Examples is clothing: square pockets, checks, plaids necklines, yokes, collars, cuffs.

overcast edge (stitch). The edge of a piece of fabric that has been sewn with an overcast stitch. An overcast hand stitch is a stitch used for finishing the raw edges of fabric to prevent them from raveling. (Working from either direction, take diagonal stitches over the edge, spacing them an even distance apart at a uniform depth.) The same as a zigzag stitch on the sewing machine.

pill. To form into small pill-like balls as the fuzz on a wool sweater.

protein. Organic nitrogen containing compound synthesized by plants and animals.

radial arrangement. Lines emerge from a central point. Examples in clothing: when gathers, tucks, seams, darts, flowing lines or colors, emerge from a central point.

seam-binding. A straight tape used for finishing hem edges; comes in woven or lace form.

silhouette. A drawing consisting of the outline of something and filled in with a solid color.

subordinates. To be made inferior or of less importance.

synonymously. Expressing or implying the same idea.

synthetic. Pertaining to compounds formed by chemical reactions in a laboratory, as opposed to those of natural origin.

transition. When a curved line leads the eye over an angle. Examples in clothing: dropped shoulder, puffed sleeves, scarves, shawls.

transparent monofilament. A clear, single large filament of synthetic fiber.

turned under. Hem edge is turned under to form a fold in the slipstitch method of hemming.

uniforms. Outfits or articles of clothing that are alike and specific to everyone in a certain group of individuals.

utilitarian. Having regard to usefulness rather than beauty ornamentation, etc.

values. Ideas, beliefs, or things that are important to a person.

BIBLIOGRAPHY

Compton's Encyclopedia Online, "Clothing;" "Fashion;" "Dress Design."

Packer, J.I., Tenney, Merrill C. and White, William Jr., *The Bible Almanac*, Thomas Nelson Publishers, Tennessee, 1980.

Reader's Digest Complete Guide to Sewing, 11th printing, The Reader's Digest Association, Inc., New York, 1985.

Singer Sewing Reference Library, *Clothing Care and Repair*, Cy DeCrosse Incorporated, Minnesota, 1985.

The Vogue Sewing Book, Butterick Publishing, New York, 1980.

Wagenvoord, James, *Personal Style, The Man's Guide to Fashion Fitness, Travel and Entertaining*, Holt, Rinehart and Winston, New York, 1985.

Before taking the LIFEPAC Test, you may want to do one or more of these self checks.

1. _____ Read the objectives. Check to see if you can do them.

2. _____ Restudy the material related to any objectives that you cannot do.

3. _____ Use the SQ3R study procedure to review the material.

4. _____ Review activities, Self Tests and LIFEPAC vocabulary words.

5. _____ Restudy areas of weakness indicated by the last Self Test.